UNDERSTANDING AND USING
ENGLISH GRAMMAR
Second Edition

WORKBOOK Volume B

Betty Schrampfer Azar
Donald A. Azar

Chief contributor: Rachel Spack Koch
Contributors: Susan Jamieson
           Barbara Andrews
           Jeanie Francis

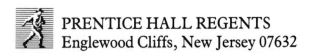
PRENTICE HALL REGENTS
Englewood Cliffs, New Jersey 07632

Editorial/production supervision: *Janet Johnston*
Interior design: *Ros Herion Freese*
Illustrations: *Don Martinetti*
Cover design: *Joel Mitnick Design*
Manufacturing buyer: *Ray Keating*

Printed in the United States of America

10 9 8 7 6 5 4 3 2 1

ISBN 0-13-944000-3

Prentice-Hall International (UK) Limited, *London*
Prentice-Hall of Australia Pty. Limited, *Sydney*
Prentice-Hall Canada Inc., *Toronto*
Prentice-Hall Hispanoamericana, S.A., *Mexico*
Prentice-Hall of India Private Limited, *New Delhi*
Prentice-Hall of Japan, Inc., *Tokyo*
Simon & Schuster Asia Pte. Ltd., *Singapore*
Editora Prentice-Hall do Brasil, Ltda., *Rio de Janeiro*

To Chelsea,
with all our love.

Contents

Chapter 6 ADJECTIVE CLAUSES

Chapter 7 NOUN CLAUSES

Chapter 8   SHOWING RELATIONSHIPS BETWEEN IDEAS—PART I

Chapter 9 SHOWING RELATIONSHIPS BETWEEN IDEAS—PART II

Chapter 10 CONDITIONAL SENTENCES

PRACTICE	PAGE

Preface

This ESL grammar workbook accompanies *Understanding and Using English Grammar (Second Edition)*. It is a place for students to explore and practice structures on their own. At the same time, the workbook provides supplementary teaching materials for the teacher to select as needed. The exercises are designated (1) SELFSTUDY PRACTICES or (2) GUIDED STUDY PRACTICES:

(1) The SELFSTUDY PRACTICES are designed for independent out-of-class use by the students, who can correct their own work by referring to the Answer Key Booklet at the back of the workbook. The SELFSTUDY PRACTICES allow students ample opportunities to clarify their understandings, explore structures at their own pace, assess their proficiency, and expand their usage ability as well as their vocabulary.

(2) The GUIDED STUDY PRACTICES, for which the answers are not given, are intended primarily as additional material for the teacher to use as s/he sees the need. They can be used for classwork, homework, or individualized instruction.

The content of the exercises often seeks to inform, challenge, and pique the curiosity of students as they practice their English language skills. In addition, the workbook contains suggestions for various language-learning activities such as discussions, games, and writing topics.

There are two workbooks. *Workbook Volume A* has exercises for Chapters 1–4 and Appendix 1. *Workbook Volume B* contains exercises for Chapters 5–10. The workbooks are coordinated with the main text. The heading for each practice refers the students to the charts in the main text that contain explanations of the grammar being practiced. The *Teacher's Guide* that accompanies the main text includes suggestions for using the workbooks, plus answers to the GUIDED STUDY PRACTICES.

The answer key to the SELFSTUDY PRACTICES is on perforated pages. The students can remove it to construct their own separate Answer Key Booklet. The students can write in the workbook and then place the Answer Key Booklet next to the workbook to make it easy for them to correct their answers.

Acknowledgments

My thanks go to all who have made this project possible. First of all to Don, an experienced ESL teacher and administrator, who at my urging turned his hand to writing. The enjoyment he took in his task is evident in the lively spirit of the workbook.

I also thank the contributors—Shelley Koch, Susan Jamieson, Jeanie Francis, and Barbara Andrews—for the wonderful materials they provided us to work with. They are experienced teachers who understand their students. Their understandings have greatly enhanced the workbook.

My mom and dad are also due great thanks. My mom keyboards and holds me to account for every word and punctuation mark, and my dad contributes a plethora of ideas for contexts. My thanks also to Chelsea for her help in the office and to Joy Edwards for her able and valued assistance.

And, of course, no book is possible without thoughtful editors: thanks go to Tina Carver, Ros Herion, Sylvia Moore, Janet Johnston—and all the support circle at Prentice Hall Regents.

BETTY S. AZAR
Langley, Washington

First, foremost, and above all, I want to express my appreciation to Betty. Although we worked together teaching ESL for many years, collaboration on this writing project brought our work lives together in a very different way. Her patience, her guidance, and her incredible expertise kept me from roaming too far afield from our objective. She taught me a great deal.

I also want to express my gratitude to our contributing writers: Rachel Spack (Shelley) Koch, Susan Jamieson, Barbara Andrews, and Jeanie Francis. They worked with me in developing draft material and did their part well. I also thank them for adapting to any inconsistencies in communications and schedule.

And finally, there's Chelsea Parker. She went through it all with us, and she'll have to do it again. Our work, and we, are all the better for that.

DONALD A. AZAR
Langley, Washington

CHAPTER 5
Singular and Plural

◇ **PRACTICE 1—SELFSTUDY: Final -s/-es. (Charts 5-1 and 5-2)**

Directions: Add final *-s/-es* where necessary. Do not change, add, or omit any other words in the sentences.

       cares   feathers
1. A bird care for its feather by cleaning them with its beak.

2. There are many occupation in the world. Doctor take care of sick people. Pilot fly airplane. Farmer raise crop. Shepherd herd sheep.

3. An architect design building. An archeologist dig in the ground to find object from past civilizations.

4. The first modern computer were developed in the 1930s and 1940s. Computer were not commercially available until the 1950s.

5. There are several factory in my hometown. The glass factory employ many people.

6. Kangaroo are Australian animal. They are not found on any of the other continent, except in zoo.

7. Mosquito are found everywhere in the world, including the Arctic.

8. At one time, many people believed that tomato were poisonous.

9. Bird, fish, insect, and mammal are different species. Each group of these life form shares physical characteristic.

10. Most of the creature in the world possess the five sense of sight, hearing, touch, taste, and smell. However, these sense are often more highly developed in one species than another. Bird have a highly developed sense of sight. For instance, an eagle can spot a small lizard from high in the air. The lizard would be undetectable by a human being from the same distance. Animal that hunt by following a trail on the ground may have poor eyesight but a keen sense of smell. For example, dog see a blurred, gray world because they are nearsighted and cannot see colors. However, they can smell thousands of times better than human being can.

◇ **PRACTICE 2—SELFSTUDY: Plural nouns. (Charts 5-1 and 5-2)**

Directions: Write the correct form of the nouns in parentheses.

1. I met some interesting _____**men**_____ at the meeting last night. (*man*)

2. The farmer loaded his cart with _____**boxes**_____ of fresh vegetables to take to market.

   His cart was pulled by two _____**oxen**_____. (*box, ox*)

3. The baby got two new _____. (*tooth*)

4. I need some _____ to light the fire. (*match*)

5. Alex saw some _____

   running across the floor. (*mouse*)

6. We cooked some _____ for dinner. (*potato*)

7. The north side of the island has no _____. There are only steep

   _____. No one can climb these steep walls of rock. (*beach, cliff*)

8. If a houseplant is given too much water, its lower _____ turn yellow. (*leaf*)

9. Before Marie signed the contract, she talked to two _____. (*attorney*)

10. New scientific _____ are made every day in _____ throughout

    the world. (*discovery, laboratory*)

11. I caught several _____ in the lake. (*fish*)

12. On our trip in the mountains, we saw some _____, _____,

    _____, and wild _____. (*wolf, fox, deer, sheep*)

13. When the _____ were playing a game, they hid behind some

    _____. (*child, bush*)

14. When I was at the park, I saw some _____ and _____

    swimming in a pond. (*duck, goose*)

15. When we spoke in the cave, we could hear _____ of our voices. (*echo*)

16. The music building at the university has 27 _____. Students need to sign up

    for practice times. (*piano*)

◇ PRACTICE 3—SELFSTUDY: Irregular foreign plurals. (Chart 5-2)

Directions: Use the correct plural form of the nouns in the list to complete the sentences. Use each word only one time.

bacterium	curriculum	medium	phenomenon
crisis	datum	memorandum	stimulus
criterion	hypothesis	oasis	✔ thesis

1. Graduate students are often required to write long papers in which they state an opinion and give evidence to support it. These papers are often referred to as _____**theses**_____.

2. Thunder and lightning are _____ of nature.

3. Before the students began their chemistry experiments, they stated theories to explain what was going to happen in their experiments. In other words, they made _____.

4. The government of that country is unstable. The country has faced many political _____ in the last ten years. It has had to face one problem after another.

5. The office supervisor, Ms. Hall, is well known for the large number of _____ she sends to her staff. She believes it is necessary to write many notes to remind the staff of things that need to be taken care of.

6. People get most of their news about the world through the mass _____ (that is, through radio, television, newspapers, and magazines).

7. The teacher wanted to make sure the students understood the standards by which she would make her judgments. She carefully explained the _____ she would use to judge the students' work.

8. All of the departments at the university provide descriptions of their _____ in the school catalog. Look there to find out what courses the departments offer.

9. Certain factors cause plants to grow. These _____ are light, water, and fertile soil.

10. Very small living things that can cause disease are called germs. Germs are forms of _____.

11. In a desert, there are places where water is available and a few plants grow. These areas are called _____.

12. The researcher assembled numerous facts through months of investigation. She used the _____ she had gathered to write a report for a scientific journal.*

◇ PRACTICE 4—SELFSTUDY: Possessive nouns. (Chart 5-3)

Directions: Make the italicized nouns possessive by adding *apostrophes* and final *-s/-es* as necessary.

1. I enjoy visiting *friend* **s'** houses.

2. When I was in Chicago, I stayed at a *friend* **'s** house.

---

*In very formal English, *data* is considered plural, but more typically it is used as a singular noncount noun.
Typical use: *This data is not correct.* Formal use: *These data are not correct.*

3. My uncle is my *father*   brother.

4. I have four aunts. All of my *aunt*   homes are within walking distance of my *mother*   apartment.

5. Tom's *aunt*   oldest son is a violinist.

6. There were five astronauts aboard the space shuttle. The *astronaut*   safe return to earth was a welcome sight to millions of television viewers.

7. The *children*   favorite part of the circus was the elephant act.

8. When the *child*   toy broke, I fixed it.

9. I borrowed the *secretary*   pen to finish filling out the application form.

10. It is the *people*   right to know what the city is going to do about the housing problem.

11. *Bill*   wife is a factory worker.

12. *Bess*   husband is a housepainter.

13. There are quite a few diplomats in the city. Almost all of the *diplomat*   children attend a special school.

14. A *diplomat*   work almost invariably involves extensive traveling.

◇ **PRACTICE 5—SELFSTUDY: Using apostrophes.**
                 (Chart 5-3; Appendix 1, Charts A-7 and A-8)

Directions: Add apostrophes as necessary to mark a possessive noun or a contraction.

    Mary's   ***He's***
1. ~~Marys~~ father works at the Northgate Medical Center. ~~Hes~~ a dentist.

2. Jacks parents live in Georgia. His parents home is in Atlanta.

3. Our teachers last name is Wells. Shes one of the best teachers in the school.

4. Our teachers last names are Wells, Hunt, and Moore. Theyre all good teachers.

5. Ms. Wells husband is also a teacher. Ms. Hunts husband is an engineer.

6. Its well known that a bear likes sweet food. Its favorite food is honey.

7. Anns telephone number is 555-8989. Ours is 555–9898. People often confuse hers with ours, so we get frequent calls for her.

8. The tiger is a beautiful animal. Its coat is orange and white with black stripes. Although its found in the wild only in Asia, people throughout the world appreciate its beauty and power. Even though tigers are protected by laws, many scientists predict their extinction within twenty to thirty years. How much poorer our childrens and grandchildrens lives will be when the earth no longer has a place for tigers, elephants, wolves, and numerous other animals whose fates rely upon the wisdom and compassion of humankind.

◇ PRACTICE 6—GUIDED STUDY: Using apostrophes.
　　　　　　　　　　　　　　(Chart 5-3; Appendix 1, Charts A-7 and A-8)

Directions: Add apostrophes as necessary to mark a possessive noun or a contraction.

1. A polar bears sense of smell is keen. Its ability to smell prey over a mile away is important to
   its survival in the vast expanses of snow and ice where it lives.

2. Texas is a leading producer of petroleum and natural gas. Its one of the worlds largest storage
   areas for petroleum.

3. All of the performers in the play did well. The audience applauded the actors excellent
   performance.

4. Psychologists have developed many different kinds of tests. A "personality test" is used to
   evaluate an individuals personal characteristics, such as friendliness or trustworthiness.

5. Many mythological stories tell of heroes encounters with giants or dangerous animals. In one
   story, the heros encounter with a dragon saves a village from destruction.

6. Childrens play is an important part of their lives. It teaches them about their environment
   while theyre having fun. For instance, they can learn that boats float and can practice ways to
   make boats move across water. Toys are not limited to children. Adults have their own toys,
   such as pleasure boats, and children have theirs, such as miniature boats. Adults toys are
   usually much more expensive than childrens toys.

◇ PRACTICE 7—SELFSTUDY: Using nouns as modifiers. (Chart 5-4)

Directions: Complete the sentences with the nouns in the parentheses. Use the singular or plural
form as appropriate.

1. They sell _____*shoes*_____ at that store. It is a _____*shoe*_____ store. (*shoe*)

2. I like _____ salads. I like salads that contain _____. (*tomato*)

3. This soup is made from black _____. It is black _____ soup. (*bean*)

4. People can buy special food in small jars for _____. It is called _____
   food. (*baby*)

5. I have a _____ garden. I grow many different kinds of
   _____. (*vegetable*)

6. Some people are addicted to _____. They are _____ addicts. (*drug*)

7. In tropical climates, sometimes it is necessary to hang a net over a bed to protect the sleeper
   from _____. It is called a _____ net. (*mosquito*)

8. At a formal dinner, there are usually two forks on the table. The smaller fork is for
   _____. It is a _____ fork. (*salad*)

◇ PRACTICE 8—SELFSTUDY: Using nouns as modifiers. (Chart 5-4)

Directions: Complete the sentences with the words in parentheses. Use the singular or plural form as appropriate. Include hyphens (-) as necessary.

1. (*two + hour*) The plane was late. We had a _____**two-hour**_____ wait. We had to wait for _____**two hours**_____.

2. (*ten + year + old*) My brother is _____**ten years old**_____. I have a _____**ten-year-old**_____ brother.

3. (*two + lane*) We drove down an old, narrow highway that had only _____. We drove down a _____ highway.

4. (*five + minute*) I gave a _____ speech in class. My speech lasted for _____.

5. (*sixty + year + old*) The Watkins live in a _____ house. Any house that is _____ usually needs a lot of repairs.

6. (*ten + speed*) Joe can shift his bicycle into _____ different _____. He has a _____ bike.

7. (*six + game*) The basketball team has won _____ in a row (i.e., they haven't lost one of their last six games). They have a _____ winning streak.

8. (*three + letter*) "Arm" and "dog" are _____ words. Each of them has _____.

◇ PRACTICE 9—SELFSTUDY: Using nouns as modifiers. (Chart 5-4)

Directions: What do you call the following?

1. someone who robs banks → *a bank robber*
2. someone who fights bulls → *a bullfighter**
3. someone who collects stamps → *a stamp collector†*

4. someone who trains animals
5. someone who tells stories*
6. someone who collects taxes†
7. something that opens cans
8. something that wipes a windshield
9. someone who earns wages
10. someone who manages an office
11. someone who programs computers
12. someone who keeps books*

13. something that removes spots
14. something that holds pots
15. someone who makes trouble*
16. someone who reads minds
17. something that dries hair
18. something that peels potatoes
19. someone who plays tennis
20. someone who fights fires*
21. someone who carries mail

_____
*Usually spelled as one word.
†Spelled with *-or* instead of *-er*.

Directions: Add *a/an* if necessary. Write ø in the blank if the noun is noncount. Capitalize as appropriate.

1. __*A*__ *bird* has wings.

2. __*An*__ *animal* needs a regular supply of food.

3. __*ø F*__ *food* is a necessity of life.

4. _____ *concert* is a musical performance.

5. _____ *opera* is a musical play.

6. _____ *music* consists of a series of pleasant sounds.

7. _____ *cup* is a small container used for liquids.

8. _____ *milk* is nutritious.

9. _____ *island* is a piece of land surrounded by water.

10. _____ *gold* is a metal.

11. _____ *bridge* is a structure that spans a river.

12. _____ *valley* is an area of land between two mountains.

13. _____ *health* is one of the most important things in life.

14. _____ *adjective* is a word that modifies a noun.

15. _____ *knowledge* is a source of power.

16. _____ *golf* is a sport.

17. _____ *professional golfer* has to practice long hours.

18. _____ *tree* needs water to survive.

19. _____ *water* is composed of oxygen and hydrogen.

20. _____ *homework* is a necessary part of a course of study.

21. _____ *grammar* is interesting and fun.

22. _____ *sentence* usually contains a subject and a verb.

23. _____ *English* is used in airports throughout much of the world.

24. _____ *leaf* is green until it begins to die.

25. _____ *orange* is green until it ripens.

26. _____ *fruit* is good for you.

27. _____ *iron* is a metal.

28. _____ *iron* is an instrument used to take wrinkles out of clothes.

29. _____ *basketball* is round.

30. _____ *basketball* is a sport.

◇ **PRACTICE 11—SELFSTUDY:** Count and noncount nouns.
(Charts 5-5 → 5-7; Appendix 1, Charts E-1 and E-2)

Directions: Use *a/an* or *some* in the following:

1. The teacher made _____*an*_____ announcement.

2. I saw _____*a*_____ bird.

3. I saw _____*some*_____ birds.

4. She borrowed _____*some*_____ money from her uncle.

5. I had _____ accident.

6. I have _____ homework to do tonight.

7. There is _____ table in the room.

8. There is _____ furniture in the room.

9. There are _____ chairs in the room.

10. My father gave me _____ advice.

11. She is carrying _____ suitcase.

12. She is carrying _____ luggage.

13. There was _____ earthquake in California.

14. I got _____ letters in the mail.

15. Ann got _____ letter from her mother.

16. Jerry got _____ mail yesterday.

17. A computer is _____ machine that can solve problems.

18. The factory bought _____ new machinery.

19. _____ machines are powered by electricity. Some use other sources of energy.

20. I threw away _____ junk.

21. I threw away _____ old basket that was falling apart.

22. I threw away _____ old boots that had holes in them.

◇ **PRACTICE 12—GUIDED STUDY:** Count and noncount nouns. (Charts 5-5 → 5-7)

Directions: A favorite game for adults and children alike is called "My Grandfather's Store." It is played with a group of people. Each person begins his/her turn by saying, "*I went to my grandfather's store and bought. . . .*" The first person names something that begins with the letter "A." The second person repeats what the first person said, and then names something that begins with the letter "B." The game continues to the letter "Z," the end of the alphabet. The people in the group have to listen carefully and remember all the items previously named.

Example:

1st person: *I went to my grandfather's store and bought **an apple**.*
2nd person: *I went to my grandfather's store and bought **an apple** and **some bread**.*
3rd person: *I went to my grandfather's store and bought **an apple, some bread,** and **a camel**.*
4th person: *I went to my grandfather's store and bought **an apple, some bread, a camel,** and **some dark socks**.*
5th person: *Etc.*

Assume that "grandfather's store" sells just about anything anyone would ever think of. Pay special attention to the use of *a, an,* and *some.*

Alternative beginnings:
Tomorrow I'm going to (name of a place). In my suitcase, I will pack . . . .
If I lived on a deserted island, I would need . . . .

◇ PRACTICE 13—SELFSTUDY: Count and noncount nouns. (Charts 5-5 → 5-7)

Directions: Add final *-s/-es* to the italicized nouns if necessary.

(no change)
1. Jackie has brown *hair* and gray *eyes* .

2. My parents gave me some good *advice* .

3. I always drink *water* when I'm hot and thirsty.

4. We ate some *sandwich* for lunch.

5. We've been having some bad *weather* lately.

6. I have a lot of *homework* to do tonight.

7. Maria took some good *photograph* at the wedding party.

8. Our country has made a lot of *progress* in the last 25 years.

9. That book has a lot of good *idea* .

10. An encyclopedia contains a lot of *information* .

11. I've learned a lot of new *vocabulary* .

12. Olga knows a lot of American *slang* .

13. Every day, I learn some more new *word* in English.

14. A gambler needs a lot of *luck* .

15. Pioneer women had a lot of *courage* .

16. We bought some new *clothing* .

17. I bought a pair of leather *glove* .

18. At rush hour there are a lot of *car* on the highway. Although normally it takes us twenty *minute* to drive from home to work, at rush hour it can take an hour because of the heavy *traffic* .

19. We received a postcard from Melissa today. She's on vacation in the country, staying in a two-hundred-*year* -old inn. She says the area has fantastic *scenery* and that there hasn't been any *rain* , although there is *fog* in the mornings. She's been playing a lot of tennis and *golf* during the day, and *bridge* at night. She's having a lot of *fun* .

20. *Traveling* can impart a great deal of *education* as well as *enjoyment* . When *people* travel to another *country* , they can learn about its *history* , *economy* , and *architecture* , as well as become acquainted with its various *custom* .

◇ **PRACTICE 14—GUIDED STUDY: Count and noncount nouns. (Charts 5-1 → 5-7)**

Directions: Add final *-s/-es* to the italicized nouns if necessary. Do not add, omit, or change any other words.

(no change)

1. I like to experience different *season***s** . I like both hot and cold *weather* .

2. Being a parent has brought me a lot of *happiness* . Parenting requires a lot of *patience* , but it provides many *reward* .

3. *Butterfly* begin as *caterpillar* and then are transformed into beautiful *insect* with vividly colored *wing* .

4. Although everyone believed the accused man was guilty of murder, he was acquitted. The prosecuting attorney did not have enough *evidence* to convict him, nor even any *proof* that he had been able to enter the murdered man's house.

5. You need more *calcium* in your diet, Mrs. Abbott. It is found in *milk* and milk *product* , in dark green *vegetable* such as *broccoli* , and in *fish* such as *sardine* . You need *vitamin* , too. Do you take *vitamin* *pill* ?

6. I don't mind hard *work* , but the *job* that I have now is too stressful. I'm going to look for another *position* . *Unemployment* in my field is low now, so there should be plenty of *job* for me to choose from.

7. Last night we heard about a new political *crisis* in our country. Do you have any more *information* about it? Are there any reports of *violence* ? We've heard a lot of rumors about what may be happening, but we're anxious to know the *truth* . We need *fact* , not *gossip* .

8. Experienced *traveler* learn to travel with minimal *luggage* . My globe-trotting aunt can pack everything she needs into two small *suitcase* , whether a trip will last for three *day* or three *month* . I'm not an experienced *traveler* . When I travel, I invariably take along too much *stuff* . Last month I took a three-*day* trip to Chicago and had twice as many clothes as I needed.

◇ **PRACTICE 15—SELFSTUDY: *Much* vs. *many*. (Charts 5-1 → 5-8)**

Directions: Write *much* or *many*. Also write the plural form of the italicized nouns as necessary. In some sentences, you will need to choose the correct verb in parentheses.

1. I haven't visited _____**many**_____ *city* **cities** in the United States.

2. I don't have _____**much**_____ *money* .

3. There (is/are) _____**is**_____ too _____**much**_____ *furniture* in our living room.

4. There (isn't/aren't) _____**aren't**_____ _____**many**_____ *hotel* **hotels** in my hometown.

5. I haven't gotten _____ *mail* lately.

6. I don't get _____ letter .

7. There (isn't/aren't) _____ _____ traffic today.

8. There (isn't/aren't) _____ _____ car on the road today.

9. I can't go with you because I have too _____ work to do.

10. How _____ side does a pentagon have?*

11. I couldn't find _____ information in that book.

12. How _____ homework did the teacher assign?

13. I haven't met _____ people since I came here.

14. How _____ postage do I need to mail this letter?

15. I think there (is/are) _____ too _____ violence on television.

16. I don't have _____ patience with incompetence.

17. The doctor has so _____ patient that she has to work at least 12 hours a day.

18. How _____ tooth does the average person have?*

19. There (isn't/aren't) _____ _____ international news in the local paper.

20. How _____ fish (is/are) _____ there in the ocean?

21. How _____ continent (is/are) _____ there in the world?*

22. How _____ progress has your country made in improving the quality of medical care available to the average citizen?

◇ **PRACTICE 16—SELFSTUDY: Expressions of quantity. (Charts 5-5 → 5-8)**

Directions: If the given noun can be used to complete the sentence, write it in its correct form (singular or plural). If the given noun cannot be used to complete the sentence, write ø.

1. Helen bought several . . . .

lamp	**lamps**
furniture	ø
jewelry	ø
necklace	**necklaces**

2. Jack bought too much . . . .

shoe	ø
salt	**salt**
equipment	**equipment**
tool	ø

3. Sam bought a lot of . . . .

stamp	**stamps**
rice	**rice**
stuff	**stuff**
thing	**things**

4. Alice bought a couple of . . . .

bread	_____
loaf of bread	_____
honey	_____
jar of honey	_____

_____

*Look in the Answer Key at the back of this book for the answer to this question.

5. I read a few . . . .

    novel   _____

    literature   _____

    poem   _____

    poetry   _____

6. I bought some . . . .

    orange juice   _____

    light bulb   _____

    hardware   _____

    computer software   _____

7. We need plenty of . . . .

    sleep   _____

    information   _____

    fact   _____

    help   _____

8. I saw both . . . .

    woman   _____

    movie   _____

    scene   _____

    scenery   _____

9. He has a number of . . . .

    shirt   _____

    homework   _____

    pen   _____

    chalk   _____

10. I don't have a great deal of . . . .

    patience   _____

    wealth   _____

    friend   _____

    pencil   _____

11. I need a little . . . .

    luck   _____

    money   _____

    advice   _____

    new hat   _____

12. The author has many . . . .

    idea   _____

    theory   _____

    hypothesis   _____

    knowledge   _____

◇ PRACTICE 17—SELFSTUDY: Using *a few/few; a little/little.* (Chart 5-9)

Directions: Without substantially changing the meaning of the sentence, replace the italicized words with **a few, (very) few, a little,** or **(very) little.**

        a little

1. I think that *some* lemon juice on fish makes it taste better.

           (very) few

2. Many people are multilingual, but *not many* people speak more than ten languages.

3. *Some* sunshine is better than none.

4. January is a cold and dreary month in the northern states. There is *not much* sunshine during that month.

5. My parents like to watch TV. Every evening they watch *two or three* programs on TV before they go to bed.

6. I don't watch TV very much because there are *hardly any* television programs that I enjoy.

7. If a door squeaks, *several* drops of oil in the right places can prevent future trouble.

8. If your door squeaks, put *some* oil on the hinges.

9. Mr. Adams doesn't like to wear rings on his fingers. He wears *almost no* jewelry.

10. You might reach your goal if you put forth *some* more effort.

11. Even though the mountain is very steep and the climb is hazardous, *several* strong-willed people have managed to reach the top.

12. The number of people in the world who are willing to risk their lives climbing a dangerous mountain is small. *Not very many* people will actually face death to climb a mountain.

◇ **PRACTICE 18—SELFSTUDY: Using *of* in expressions of quantity. (Chart 5-10)**

Directions: Add *of* or write ø.

1. When I went shopping yesterday, there were several _____ø_____ jackets in my size.

2. Several _____*of*_____ the jackets were made of 100 percent wool.

3. Many _____ students work part-time while they are attending school.

4. Many _____ my classmates have part-time jobs.

5. Some _____ dairy products are high in cholesterol.

6. Some _____ my favorite kinds of food are not good for me to eat.

7. The teacher didn't fail any _____ the students in his class.

8. Any _____ passengers who have first-class tickets can board the plane first.

9. I picked a few _____ flowers from my garden and made a bouquet.

10. A few _____ the flowers in the bouquet have already wilted.

11. Everyone needs a little _____ luck in life.

12. Most _____ babies learn to walk before their first birthday.

13. Our company imports products from abroad. Most _____ these new products are testmarketed in selected cities.

14. Most _____ people enjoy picnics.

15. Some _____ the people we want to invite for our anniversary dinner will be on vacation.

16. Not all _____ trees lose their leaves in winter.

17. All _____ deciduous trees lose their leaves during the cold part of the year, whereas evergreen trees do not.

18. All _____ the trees in that orchard have been sprayed with pesticides.

19. Both _____ my sisters attended Harvard University.

20. Both _____ women are talented in music and drama.

21. The concert was delayed because two _____ the musicians had left their instruments on the bus.

22. A trio consists of three _____ musicians.

23. I have two _____ sisters and three _____ brothers.

24. Two _____ my brothers live in St. Louis.

25. A hundred _____ people bought tickets to the lecture.

26. Two hundred _____ people came to the public meeting.

27. Hundreds _____ people visit the Lincoln Memorial every day.

28. A thousand _____ years ago, the power of electricity had not been discovered.

29. Three thousand _____ years ago, the number of planets in our solar system was unknown.

30. Thousands _____ years ago, the wheel was invented.

◇ **PRACTICE 19—GUIDED STUDY: Using *of* in expressions of quantity. (Chart 5-10)**

Directions: Add *of* or write ∅.

1. Some _____∅_____ fish are surface feeders. Others are bottom feeders.

2. Some _____*of*_____ the fish we caught were too small to keep.

3. Almost all ___*of* OR: ∅___ the fish in Jennifer's aquarium died. She finally had to admit that she didn't know much about taking care of tropical fish.

4. I bought several _____ books at the used book sale.

5. Several _____ my friends and I have volunteered to clean up the litter left on the school grounds by thoughtless students.

6. A few _____ children are given their first watch by the time they are six years old. However, most _____ these children cannot tell time correctly.

7. When my parents were young, they had little _____ opportunity to travel.

8. Square dancing is a traditional folk dance in the United States. We all had a lot _____ fun learning to square dance at the party. Many _____ the people at the party had never done any square dancing before.

9. The airline was crippled by a strike last month, but now it's over. All _____ the pilots were happy to get back to work after the strike.

10. Most _____ people have a little _____ trouble using the currency in a foreign country for a few _____ days after they first arrive.

11. There's nothing I like better than a good book, but I haven't done much _____ reading for fun lately. Most _____ the reading I do is related to my work.

12. It's important for young people to have goals in their lives. My mother always told me that any _____ dream is worth pursuing if I know in my heart it is what I want to do. Few _____ people have made great accomplishments in life without first having a dream—a personal, inner vision of what is possible.

◇ PRACTICE 20—GUIDED STUDY: Writing.

Directions: In writing, describe your future. What are your goals and how are you going to reach them?

◇ PRACTICE 21—SELFSTUDY: Using *one, each, every.* (Chart 5-11)

Directions: Choose the correct word in italics.

1. Each (*student,*) *students* in the class is required to take the final examination.
2. Each of the *student,* (*students*) in the class is required to take the final examination.
3. There is at least one window in every *room, rooms* in our apartment.
4. Every one of the *room, rooms* in our apartment has at least one window.
5. My bedroom has only one, very small *window, windows* .
6. One of the smallest *window, windows* in our apartment is in my bedroom.
7. When John bought some supplies at the hardware store, he thought the total amount on the bill was incorrect, so he checked each *item, items* on his bill very carefully.
8. Each of the *item, items* on the bill was correct.
9. Susan has traveled widely, but she has visited only one Scandinavian *country, countries* .
10. Alex took an extended vacation in northern Europe last summer. Sweden was one of the *country, countries* he visited when he was in Scandinavia.
11. Tom believes that there are no strangers. He views each *person, people* in the world as a friend he hasn't met yet.
12. I answered every *question, questions* on the examination. I didn't skip any.
13. Each one of the *child, children* in the class was given a piece of paper and a crayon. Each *child, children* drew a picture.
14. Hunger is one of the biggest *problem, problems* in the world today.
15. Each of the *applicant, applicants* for the scholarship is required to furnish five references (that is, names of people who are willing to write letters of recommendation).

◇ PRACTICE 22—GUIDED STUDY: Expressions of quantity. (Charts 5-10 → 5-13)

Directions: Make each statement clearer or more accurate by adding an expression of quantity. Add other words to the sentence or make any changes you wish. The following list suggests expressions of quantity you might use.

all (of)	*many (of)*	*one (of)*	*some (of)*
each (of)	*much (of)*	*two (of)*	*several (of)*
every	*a number of*	*half of*	*(a) few (of)*
almost all (of)	*a great deal of*	*50 percent of*	*(a) little (of)*
most (of)	*a lot of*	*three-fourths of*	*hardly any (of)*
not all (of)	*plenty of*	*a majority of*	*none of*
		hundreds of	*no*

Example: My classmates speak Arabic.
Possible sentences: → Most of my classmates speak Arabic.
  → All (of) my classmates speak Arabic.
  → One of my classmates **speaks** Arabic.
  → Hardly any of my classmates speak Arabic.
  → None of my classmates **speaks** Arabic.

1. The people in my class are international students.

2. People are friendly.

3. The pages in this book contain illustrations.

4. Babies are born bald.

5. The students in my class are from South America.

6. People like to live alone.

7. The people I know like to live alone.

8. The countries in the world are in the northern hemisphere.

9. The citizens of the United States speak English.

10. Children like to read scary stories.

11. The children in my country go to school.

12. Airplanes depart and arrive precisely on time.

13. The rivers in the world are polluted.

14. The pollution in the world today is caused by human beings.

15. City dwellers do not have cars.

16. The food at (*the name of the place you usually eat*) is very good.

◇ PRACTICE 23—SELFSTUDY: Subject-verb agreement. (Charts 5-12 → 5-15)

Directions: Choose the correct completion for the sentence.

1. Most of the mountain peaks in the Himalayan range   *is,* (*are*) covered with snow the year around.

2. Nearly 40 percent of the people in our town never   *votes, vote*   in local elections.

3. A number of students   *has, have*   participated in intensive language programs abroad.

4. The number of students who knew the answer to the last question on the exam *was, were* very low.

5. Studying a foreign language often *leads, lead* students to learn about the culture of the countries where it is spoken.

6. The United States of America *consists, consist* of fifty separate states.

7. Two hours *is, are* too long to wait, don't you think?

8. *Isn't, Aren't* Portuguese spoken in Brazil?

9. A lot of Brazilians *speaks and understands, speak and understand* Spanish.

10. Why *is, are* the police standing over there?

11. Why *does, do* most of the television stations broadcast national news at the same hour?

12. Some of the most important books for my report *is, are* not available in the school library.

13. There *has, have* been times when I have seriously considered dropping out of school.

14. Not one of the men in the original group of U.S. astronauts *continues, continue* in the space program today.

15. The news on the radio and TV stations *confirms, confirm* that a serious storm is approaching our city.

16. Geography *is, are* fascinating. Mathematics *is, are* fascinating.

17. Mathematics and geography *is, are* my favorite subjects.

18. All of the windows in our house *was, were* broken in the earthquake.

19. By law, every man, woman, and child *is, are* guaranteed the right to free speech.

20. Some of the movie about the creatures from outer space *was, were* surprisingly funny.

21. Some of the movies these days *contains, contain* too much violence.

22. *Is, Are* pineapple and sugar the leading crops in Hawaii today?

23. Why *is, are* there a shortage of certified school teachers at the present time?

24. How many people *is, are* there in Canada?*

25. What *is, are* the population of Canada?*

26. How many of the states in the United States *begins, begin* with the letter "A"?*

27. Which one of the continents in the world *is, are* uninhabited?*

28. Most of the water in the world is salt water. What percentage of the water in the world *is, are* fresh water?*

29. The most common name for dogs in the United States *is, are* "Rover."

30. What places in the world *has, have* no snakes?*

---

*Look in the Answer Key for the answer to this question.

◇ PRACTICE 24—GUIDED STUDY: Subject-verb agreement. (Charts 5-12 → 5-15)

Directions: Choose the correct completion for the sentence.

1. A lot of the books in my office   *is,* (*are*)   very valuable to me.

2. A lot of the advice my grandparents gave me   *has, have*   proven to be invaluable.

3. All of the employees in that company   *is, are*   required to be proficient in a second language.

4. Listening to very loud music at rock concerts   *has, have*   caused hearing loss in some teenagers.

5. Many of the satellites orbiting the earth   *is, are*   used for communications.

6. The news about the long-range effects of pollution   *is, are*   disturbing.

7. *Doesn't, Don't*   everybody   *seeks, seek*   peace and contentment in life?

8. According to the poll, 53 percent of the people in the country   *doesn't, don't*   want the incumbent to be re-elected.

9. Even though the eye of the hurricane will miss our city, there   *is, are*   still the possibility of heavy rain and high winds.

10. Chinese   *has, have*   more than 50 thousand written characters.

11. About two-thirds of the Vietnamese   *works, work*   in agriculture.

12. A number of planes   *was, were*   delayed due to the inclement weather.

13. The number of passengers affected by the delays   *was, were*   great.

14. More men than women   *is, are*   left-handed.

15. Every girl and boy   *is, are*   required to have certain immunizations before enrolling in public school.

16. Politics   *is, are*   a constant source of interest to me.

17. Seventy-five percent of the people in New York City   *lives, live*   in upstairs apartments, not on the ground floor.

18. Most of the fish I caught   *was, were*   too small to keep for dinner.

19. Unless there   *is, are*   a profound and extensive reform of government policies in the near future, the economic conditions in that country will continue to deteriorate.

20. While I was in Paris, some of the best food I found   *was, were*   not at the well-known eating places, but in small out-of-the-way cafes.

21. *Was, Were*   there ever any doubt in your mind about the outcome of the election?

22. Where   *is, are*   my gloves? Have you seen them anywhere? I can't find them.

23. Where   *is, are*   Kenya? Can you find it for me on the map?

24. According to one report, approximately 80 percent of all the data in computers around the world   *is, are*   in English.

◇ PRACTICE 25—SELFSTUDY: Agreement of pronouns. (Charts 5-16 → 5-20)

Directions: Complete the sentences with pronouns. In some of the blanks there is more than one possibility. Choose the appropriate singular or plural verb in parentheses where necessary.

1. A student should always hand in _____*his/her; his or her; his*_____ work on time.

2. Students should always hand in _____*their*_____ work on time.

3. Teachers determine _____ students' course of study.

4. A teacher determines _____ students' course of study.

5. Each student is expected to hand in _____ work on time.

6. All students are expected to hand in _____ work on time.

7. If anyone calls, please ask _____ to leave a message.

8. Somebody left _____ raincoat in the classroom.

9. The flight crew on our long plane trip were very attentive. _____ efforts to make us comfortable were greatly appreciated.

10. My family is wonderful. _____ (*has, have*) always helped me in any way _____ could.

11. The crowd enjoyed the game. _____ got excited whenever the home team scored.

12. The crowd at the last concert broke attendance records. _____ (*was, were*) the largest audience ever to have been in that stadium to listen to a rock concert.

◇ PRACTICE 26—SELFSTUDY: Reflexive pronouns. (Chart 5-19)

Directions: Complete the following by using appropriate reflexive pronouns.

1. John overslept and missed his plane to San Francisco. He was angry at _____*himself*_____ for not checking his alarm clock before going to bed.

2. I was a stranger at the party. I stood alone for a while, then walked over to an interesting-looking person and introduced _____.

3. Jason has only _____ to blame for the mistake he made.

4. Sue, please help _____ to some more cake. And would you like some more coffee?

5. All of you who are successful Olympic athletes should be very proud of _____. Your achievements inspire people all over the world.

6. The math team from our high school won the state competition. They should pat _____ on the back for a job well done.

7. When I was younger, I would get embarrassed by my mistakes. Now I am more relaxed and have found it is easier to laugh at _____.

8. Children need to learn to rely upon _____.

9. My father always told me to handle my problems _____ and not to expect others to solve them for me.

10. The little girl lost her teddy bear in the park. She tried to be brave, but at bedtime she cried _____ to sleep.

11. Edward lived a lonely life as a young boy. With no one to play with, he would often sit on the front steps talking to _____ or to an imaginary friend.

12. What delicious cheesecake, Amelia! Did you make this _____?

13. Whenever we have problems in life, we have to be careful not to waste too much time feeling sorry for _____.

14. After a busy day at work, I always enjoy a little time by _____.

15. Fred wanted to be able to do something unusual, so he taught _____ to drink a glass of water while standing on his head.

◇ **PRACTICE 27—SELFSTUDY: Impersonal pronouns. (Chart 5-20)**

Directions: Complete the sentences with appropriate pronouns. Choose the correct words in italics as necessary.

1. We should ask ____*ourselves*____ if ____*we are*____ (*is, are*) doing everything in _____*our*_____ power in order to solve the problem of hunger in the world.

2. Each of you should ask _____ if _____ (*is, are*) doing everything in _____ power in order to solve the problem of hunger in the world.

3. All of you should ask _____ if _____ (*is, are*) doing everything in _____ power in order to solve the problem of hunger in the world.

4. People should ask _____ if _____ (*is, are*) doing everything in _____ power in order to solve the problem of hunger in the world.

5. Everyone should ask _____ if _____ (*is, are*) doing everything in _____ power in order to solve the problem of hunger in the world.

◇ **PRACTICE 28—GUIDED STUDY: Singular-plural. (Charts 5-1 → 5-20, Appendix 1)**

Directions: Choose the correct words in italics.

1. *Penguin,* (*Penguins*) are interesting *creature,* (*creatures*) . They are *bird,* (*birds*) , but *it,* (*they*) cannot fly.

2. *Million, Millions* of *year, years* ago, they had *wing, wings* . *This, These* wings changed as the birds adapted to *its, their* environment.

3. *Penquin's, Penguins'* principal food *was, were* *fish, fishes* . They needed to be able to swim to find their food, so eventually, their *wing, wings* evolved into *flipper, flippers* that enabled them to swim through water with speed and ease.

4. Penquins *spends, spend* most of their lives in *water, waters* . However, they lay their *egg, eggs* on *land, lands* .

5. Emperor penguins have interesting *habit, habits* .

6. The female *lays, lay* one *egg, eggs* on the *ice, ices* in Arctic regions, and then immediately *returns, return* to the ocean.

7. After the female lays the egg, the male *takes, take* over. *He, They* *covers, cover* the egg with *his, their* body until *she, he, it, they* hatches.

8. *This, These* process *takes, take* 7 to 8 *week, weeks* . During *this, these* time, the male *doesn't, don't* eat.

9. After the egg *hatches, hatch* , the female returns to take care of the chick, and the male *goes, go* to the ocean to find food for *himself, herself* , his mate, and their offspring.

10. Penguins generally live in polar *region, regions* , but if you want to see them, *you, one* can go to any major zoo. Penguins seem to adapt well to life in confinement, so *you, one* can enjoy watching their antics without feeling sorry about their loss of freedom.

◇ **PRACTICE 29—SELFSTUDY: Forms of *other*. (Chart 5-21)**

Directions: Use a form of *other* to complete the sentence: ***other, another, others, the other, the others.***

1. I had a red pen, but I seem to have lost it. I guess I'd better buy _____*another*_____ one.

2. Some people are lazy. _____ are energetic. Most people are a mixture of both.

3. Two countries share the island of Hispañola. One is Haiti. _____ is the Dominican Republic.

4. Excuse me, waiter? Could you please bring me _____ fork? I dropped mine on the floor.

5. Only two countries in South America, Bolivia and Paraguay, are inland. All of _____ have coastlines.

6. Washington is one of the five states of the United States with borders on the Pacific Ocean. What are _____ states?*

7. A successful harvest depends largely on the weather. In some years, there is an abundant harvest. In _____ years, the harvest is lean, especially when there is a drought.

8. I enjoyed watching everyone at the beach. Some people were playing volleyball, while _____ were picnicking. Some were listening to music, some were sleeping, and _____ were just lying in the sun. _____ people were swimming in the surf.

9. I'll be finished with this report soon. Give me _____ twenty minutes and I'll be ready to go with you.

———————
*Look in the Answer Key for the answer to this question.

10. Ali has been here studying for almost three years. In _____ six months he will have his degree and return to his country.

11. Only three of the forty-two applicants for the job possess the necessary qualifications. None of _____ will be considered.

12. I work for Mr. Anderson every _____ Saturday. I help him with chores around his house.

◇ **PRACTICE 30—GUIDED STUDY: Forms of *other*. (Chart 5-21)**

Directions: Use a form of *other* to complete the sentence: ***other, another, others, the other, the others***.

1. Scandinavia consists of four countries. One is Denmark. _____ are Finland, Norway, and Sweden.

2. Budapest, Hungary, is actually two cities. On one side of the Danube River lies Buda, and directly across from it, on _____ side of the river, lies Pest.

3. Most of the candidates who will take the qualifying examination in May will probably pass the first time. _____ will have _____ chance next month.

4. Some people like to take vacations in the mountains. _____ prefer the seashore. Some people like to drive from place to place; _____ people prefer to get to their destinations as quickly as possible. Although many people like to travel on their vacations, many _____ prefer just to stay at home.

5. The Wolcott twins are identical. They look alike, and they think alike. Sometimes when one begins a sentence, _____ finishes it.

6. One of the most important inventions in the history of the world was the printing press. _____ was the electric light. _____ were the telephone, television, and the computer.

7. To avoid competitive disadvantages, professional boxers are classified by weight groups. There are over a dozen different weight classes. One is called the flyweight group. _____ are the featherweight, middleweight, and heavyweight groups.

8. The committee meets every _____ Monday.

9. Joe and Frank, detectives in the police department, work as a team. They work well with each _____.

10. The car I bought last year has turned out to be a real lemon! I'll never buy _____ one of the same make.

11. My report is due today, but I need _____ two days to finish it.

12. Some babies begin talking as early as six months; _____ don't speak until they are more than two years old.

◇ **PRACTICE 31—GUIDED STUDY: Forms of *other*. (Chart 5-21)**

Directions: Write sentences that include the given words. Punctuate carefully.
Examples:

I . . . two . . . one . . . (+ form of *other*) . . . .
→ *I have **two** brothers. **One** of them is in high school, and **the other** is in college.*

Some . . . like coffee . . . while (+ form of *other*) . . .
→ ***Some** people **like coffee** with their breakfasts, **while others** prefer tea.*

One city . . . (+ form of *other*) is . . . .
→ ***One city** I would like to visit is Paris. **Another is** Rome.*

1. My . . . has two . . . one of them . . . (+ form of *other*) . . . .
2. Some people . . . in their free time . . . while (+ form of *other*) . . . .
3. . . . national hero . . . (+ form of *other*) . . . .
4. . . . three . . . two of . . . (+ form of *other*) . . . .
5. . . . more time . . . (+ form of *other*) . . . minutes . . . .
6. There are three . . . that I especially like . . . one is . . . (+ form of *other*) . . . .
7. I lost . . . bought (+ form of *other*) . . . .
8. Some movies . . . while (+ form of *other*) . . . .
9. . . . speak . . . (+ form of *other*) . . . .
10. . . . is one of the longest rivers in the world . . . is (+ form of *other*) . . . .
11. Some children . . . while (+ form of *other*) . . . .
12. . . . enough money to buy . . . needed (+ form of *other*) . . . .

◇ **PRACTICE 32—SELFSTUDY: Error analysis. (Chapter 5)**

Directions: Find and correct the errors.

1. In my country, there is a lots of schools.
2. Writing compositions are very hard for me.
3. The front-page articles in the daily newspaper has the most important news.
4. Besides the zoo and the art museum, I have visited many others places in this city.
5. It's difficult for me to understand English when people uses a lot of slangs.
6. A student at the university should attend class regularly and hand in their assignments on time.
7. In the past, horses was the principal mean of transportation.
8. In my opinion, the english is a easy language to learn.
9. There is many different kind of animal in the world.
10. They want to move to other city because they don't like a cold weather.
11. I like to travel because I like to learn about other country and custom.
12. Collecting stamps is one of my hobby.
13. Chicago has many of tall skyscraper.
14. I came here three and a half month ago. I think I have made a good progress in English.
15. I was looking for my clothes, but I couldn't find it.

◇ PRACTICE 33—GUIDED STUDY: Error analysis. (Chapter 5)

Directions: Find and correct the errors.

1. When my mother was child, she lived in a small town. Now this town is big city with tall building and many highway.

2. English has borrowed quite a few of word from another languages.

3. There is many student from differents countries in my class.

4. Thousand of athlete take part in the Olympics.

5. Almost all of the house in the town are white with red roof.

6. Education is one of the most important aspect of life. Knowledges about many different things help us live fuller lives.

7. All of the students names were on the list.

8. I live in a two rooms apartment.

9. Many of people prefer to live in small towns. Their attachment to their communities prevent them from moving from place to place in search of works.

10. Todays news is just as bad as yesterdays news.

11. Almost of the students in our class speak English well.

12. The teacher gave us several homework to hand in next Tuesday.

13. Today womans work as doctor, pilot, archeologist, and many other thing. Both my mother and father are teacher's.

14. Every employees in our company respect Mr. Ward.

15. A child needs to learn how to get along with another people, how to spend his or her time wisely, and how to depend on yourself.

◇ PRACTICE 34—GUIDED STUDY: Writing.

Directions: Write a paragraph on one of the topics below. Write as quickly as you can. Write whatever comes in to your mind. Try to write 100 words in ten minutes. When you finish your paragraph, exchange it with a classmate. Correct each other's errors.

1. food   3. this room
2. English   4. animals

◇ PRACTICE TEST A—SELFSTUDY: Singular and Plural. (Chapter 5)

Directions: Choose the correct completion.
Example:
    I don't get __*B*__.
        A. *many mail*   B. *much mail*   C. *many mails*   D. *much mails*

1. The science classes at this _____ difficult.
        A. schools are   B. school is   C. school are   D. school's is

2. One of the _____ from Italy.
        A. student is   B. students are   C. student are   D. students is

3. _____ to support the case against James?
   A. Is there any proof
   B. Are there any proof
   C. Is there any proofs
   D. Are there any proofs

4. You have to pay extra if you take too _____ with you.
   A. much luggages
   B. many luggages
   C. much luggage
   D. many luggage

5. _____ in your class have tickets for the lecture series?
   A. Do any of the student
   B. Does any of the student
   C. Do any of the students
   D. Does any of the students

6. Bob got fired. It's going to be difficult for him to find _____ job.
   A. other
   B. another
   C. the other
   D. the another

7. There _____ available in his area of specialization.
   A. isn't a lot of job
   B. aren't a lot of jobs
   C. isn't a lot of jobs
   D. aren't a lot of job

8. He made the soup by mixing _____ meat with some rice.
   A. little
   B. few
   C. a little
   D. a few

9. Many of the _____ not expect to win.
   A. participants in the race do
   B. participant in the races does
   C. participants in the race does
   D. participant in the race does

10. The English _____ strong traditions.
    A. has many
    B. have much
    C. have many
    D. has much

11. _____ moved to that city recently.
    A. A number of Vietnamese have
    B. A number of Vietnamese has
    C. The number of Vietnamese has
    D. The number of Vietnamese have

12. Each of the reference _____ available in the school library.
    A. books on that list is
    B. books on that list are
    C. book on that list is
    D. book on that list are

13. Several _____ sleeping under a tree.
    A. of lions were
    B. lion was
    C. of the lions was
    D. lions were

14. Many of the _____ not used today. They are remnants of the past.
    A. railroad tracks around here are
    B. railroad's track around here is
    C. railroad tracks around here is
    D. railroads' tracks around here are

15. As we walked through the jungle, the _____ unusually quiet.
    A. monkeys were
    B. monkeys was
    C. monkies were
    D. monkies was

16. At the news conference, several reporters didn't get clear answers to _____ questions.
    A. theirs
    B. their
    C. his and hers
    D. his and her

17. I have a _____ sister.
    A. seven years old
    B. seven-years-old
    C. seven-year-old
    D. seven year olds

18. There _____ in the world today.
    A. is many new computer company
    B. is many new computer companies
    C. are many new computers companies
    D. are many new computer companies

19. Self-esteem is important. It's important for people to like _____.
    A. oneself
    B. yourself
    C. him/herself
    D. themselves

20. What _____ you used in picking a winner in the art contest?
    A. is the criteria
    B. are the criteria
    C. are the criterion
    D. are the criterions

Directions: Choose the correct completion.

Example:
    I don't get ___**B**___.
      A. *many mail*   B. *much mail*   C. *many mails*   D. *much mails*

1. One of the dinner ____ broken.
    A. plate is   B. plates are   C. plates is   D. plate are

2. Most ____ hard.
    A. of students work   B. students work   C. student works   D. of student works

3. Can you help me? I need ____ information.
    A. a little   B. little   C. a few   D. few

4. All of the athletes who took part in the international games should be very proud of ____.
    A. himself   B. oneself   C. themselves   D. yourselves

5. Snow and rain ____ of nature.
    A. are phenomenon   B. are phenomena   C. is phenomena   D. is phenomenon

6. I accidently broke the ____ by stepping on it. I apologized to them for my carelessness.
    A. child's toy   B. child's toys   C. children's toy   D. childrens' toys

7. Our weather is cloudy in the winter. We don't have ____.
    A. many sunshines   B. many sunshine   C. much sunshines   D. much sunshine

8. Several of my friends are ____ reporters.
    A. newspaper   B. newpapers   C. newspaper's   D. newspapers'

9. Construction workers need ____ to build a highway.
    A. an heavy equipment   B. a heavy equipment
    C. heavy equipments   D. heavy equipment

10. Our classroom is supplied with ____.
    A. plenty of chalks   B. plenty of chalk   C. several chalks   D. several chalk

11. Knowing several ____ helpful if you work for an international corporation.
    A. languages are   B. language is   C. languages is   D. language are

12. Two-thirds of my ____ from the Middle East.
    A. classmates is   B. classmate are   C. classmate is   D. classmates are

13. There ____ in my country.
    A. are a lot of problem   B. are a lot of problems
    C. is a lot of problems   D. is a lot of problem

14. Winning a lottery is a rare occurrence. ____ very small.
    A. A number of winners is   B. The number of winners is
    C. A number of winners are   D. The number of winners are

15. There are several means of mass communication. The newspaper is one. Television is ____.
    A. other   B. the other   C. another   D. the another

16. Each of the ____ own cage.
    A. birds has their   B. bird has its   C. birds have their   D. birds has its

17. I really need ____. Can we talk?
    A. some advice   B. an advice   C. some advices   D. advices

18. Every _____ a license plate.
    A. cars have   B. cars has   C. car has   D. car have

19. The swimming team has done well this year. All of _____ have trained very hard.
    A. their members   B. its members   C. it's members   D. theirs members

20. Next week, we're going to take a _____.
    A. three day trips   B. three-day trip   C. three days trip   D. three days' trip

CHAPTER 6
Adjective Clauses

◇ **PRACTICE 1—SELFSTUDY:** Basic patterns of adjective clauses. (Charts 6-1 → 6-4)

Directions: Underline the adjective clauses in the following sentences.

1. a. The paintings that are marked with a small red dot have already been sold.
   b. The paintings which are marked with a small red dot have already been sold.

2. a. The secretary who sits at the first desk on the right can give you the information.
   b. The secretary that sits at the first desk on the right can give you the information.

3. a. The shoes that I bought were made in Italy.
   b. The shoes which I bought were made in Italy.
   c. The shoes I bought were made in Italy.

4. a. I wrote a letter to the woman that I met at the meeting.
   b. I wrote a letter to the woman who(m) I met at the meeting.
   c. I wrote a letter to the woman I met at the meeting.

5. a. The speech we listened to last night was informative.
   b. The speech that we listened to last night was informative.
   c. The speech which we listened to last night was informative.
   d. The speech to which we listened last night was informative.

6. a. Dr. Jones is the professor I told you about.
   b. Dr. Jones is the professor who(m) I told you about.
   c. Dr. Jones is the professor that I told you about.
   d. Dr. Jones is the professor about whom I told you.

7. The student whose parents you just met is in one of my classes.

8. The pianist who played at the concert last night is internationally famous.

9. Some of the people a waiter has to serve at a restaurant are rude.

10. The restaurant Bob recommended was too expensive.

11. Thomas Raven is a physicist whose book on time and space has been translated into dozens of languages.

12. The woman who lives next door to us is a weathercaster on a local TV station.

◇ PRACTICE 2—SELFSTUDY: Basic patterns of adjective clauses. (Charts 6-1 → 6-4)

Directions: In the spaces, write all the pronouns possible to complete the sentence. In addition, write Ø if the sentence is correct without adding a pronoun.

1. Mr. Green is the man | *who(m)* *that* *Ø* | I was talking about.

2. She is the woman | *who* *that* | sits next to me in class.

3. The hat | | Tom is wearing is unusual.

4. Hunger and poverty are worldwide problems to | | solutions must be found.

5. I enjoyed talking with the man | | I sat next to on the plane.

6. People | | fear flying avoid traveling by plane.

7. That is the man | | daughter won the spelling bee.

8. The people about | | the novelist wrote were factory workers and their families.

9. A barrel is a large container | | is made of wood or metal.

◇ **PRACTICE 3—SELFSTUDY: Basic patterns of adjective clauses. (Charts 6-1 → 6-3)**

Directions: Write all the pronouns possible to complete the sentence. In addition, write Ø if the sentence is correct without adding a pronoun.

PART I: Using Subject Pronouns in Adjective Clauses.

1. The bat is the only mammal | **which** **that** | can fly.

2. People   [   ]   don't get enough sleep may become short-tempered and irritable.

3. The cold weather   [   ]   swept in from the north damaged the fruit crop.

4. Alex bought a bicycle   [   ]   is specially designed for long-distance racing.

5. I read about a man   [   ]   keeps chickens in his apartment.

PART II: Using Object Pronouns in Adjective Clauses.

6. We used the map | **which** **that** ø | my sister drew for us.

7. The teacher [ ] I like the most is Mrs. Grange.

8. Louise, tell us about the movie [ ] you saw last night.

9. The subject about [ ] Dr. Gold spoke was interesting.

10. The subjects [ ] we talk about in class are interesting.

11. The person to [ ] Ann spoke could not answer her question.

12. I enjoyed the people [ ] I talked to at the party.

◇ **PRACTICE 4—SELFSTUDY: Adjective clause patterns. (Charts 6-1 → 6-3)**

Directions: Combine the sentences, using all possible forms. Use (b) as an adjective clause.

1. (a) Louis knows the woman.   (b) The woman is meeting us at the airport.
   → *Louis knows the woman* { *who* / *that* } *is meeting us at the airport.*

2. (a) The chair is an antique.   (b) Sally inherited it from her grandmother.

3. (a) The bench was wet.   (b) I sat on it.

4. (a) The man finished the job in four days.   (b) I hired him to paint my house.

5. (a) I miss seeing the old woman.   (b) She used to sell flowers on that street corner.

6. (a) The architect is brilliant.   (b) Mario works with him.

7. (a) Mary tutors students. (b) They need extra help in geometry.

8. (a) I took a picture of the rainbow. (b) It appeared in the sky after the shower.

◇ **PRACTICE 5—SELFSTUDY: Adjective clauses: using *whose*. (Chart 6-4)**

Directions: Combine the sentences, using *whose* in an adjective clause.

1. The man's wife had been admitted to the hospital. I spoke to him.
   → *I spoke to the man whose wife had been admitted to the hospital.*

2. I read about the child. Her life was saved by her pet dog.
   → *I read about a child whose life was saved by her pet dog.*

3. The students raised their hands. Their names were called.

4. Jack knows a man. The man's name is William Blueheart Duckbill, Jr.

5. The woman's purse was stolen outside the supermarket. The police came to question her.

6. We live in a small town. Its inhabitants are almost invariably friendly and helpful.

7. The day care center was established to take care of children. These children's parents work during the day.

8. We couldn't find the person. His car was blocking our driveway.

9. Tobacco is a plant. Its large leaves are used for smoking or chewing.

10. Three students' reports were turned in late. The professor told them he would accept the late papers this time but never again.

◇ **PRACTICE 6—SELFSTUDY: Adjective Clauses. (Charts 6-1 → 6-4)**

Directions: Choose the correct answer or answers.

1. Yoko told me about students ___**A, D**___ have taken the entrance exam 13 times.
   A. who   B. whom   C. which   D. that

2. The secretary ___**B, C, D**___ I talked to didn't know where the meeting was.
   A. which   B. whom   C. that   D. ø

3. You need to talk to a person _____ you can trust. You will feel better if you do.
   A. whose   B. which   C. whom   D. ø

4. Bob is the kind of person to _____ one can talk about anything.
   A. who   B. whom   C. that   D. him

5. He is a person _____ friends trust him.
   A. who   B. his   C. that   D. whose

6. I'm looking for an electric can opener _____ also can sharpen knives.
   A. who   B. which   C. that   D. ø

7. People _____ live in glass houses shouldn't throw stones.*
   A. who   B. whom   C. which   D. ø

8. The problems _____ Tony has seem insurmountable.
   A. what   B. he   C. that   D. ø

_____
*This is an idiom that means: People shouldn't criticize others for faults they themselves have. For example, a lazy person shouldn't criticize another person for being lazy.

9. The man _____ I introduced you to last night may be the next president of the university.
   A. which   B. whom   C. that   D. ∅

10. Cathy is trustworthy. She's a person upon _____ you can always depend.
   A. who   B. whom   C. that   D. ∅

11. Your career should focus on a field in _____ you are genuinely interested.
   A. which   B. what   C. that   D. ∅

12. People _____ outlook on life is optimistic are usually happy people.
   A. whose   B. whom   C. that   D. which

◇ PRACTICE 7—SELFSTUDY: Adjective clauses: subject-verb agreement
   (Charts 6-1 → 6-2 and Chapter 5)

Directions: Choose the correct verb in italics.

1. There are three students in my class who *speaks, (speak)* French.

2. There is one student in my class who *speaks, speak* Greek.

3. The patients who *is, are* treated at City Hospital *doesn't, don't* need to have private physicians.

4. The courses this school *offers, offer* *is, are* listed in the catalog.

5. A pedometer is an instrument that *measures, measure* the distance a person *walks, walk*.

6. People who *suffers, suffer* from extreme shyness can sometimes overcome their problem by taking a public speaking class.

7. The boy drew pictures of people at an airport who *was, were* waiting for their planes.

8. In the months that *has, have* passed since the accident, Robert has regained the use of his legs.

9. Malnutrition and illiteracy are among the problems in the world that *has, have* no simple solutions.

10. It is estimated by those who *works, work* in the hunger program that 3500 people die from starvation in the world every day.

11. Most advertisements are directed toward adults or teenagers, but you can see commercials on television that *is, are* aimed at prompting children to persuade their parents to buy certain products.

12. The requirements of the school as written in the catalog *states, state* that all students who *wishes, wish* to attend must take an entrance exam.

◇ PRACTICE 8—SELFSTUDY: Error analysis: (Charts 6-1 → 6-4)

Directions: All of the following sentences contain errors in adjective clause structures. Correct the errors.

1. In our village, there were many people didn't have much money.

   → *In our village, there were many people who/that didn't have much money.*

   OR: *In our village, many people didn't have much money.*

2. I enjoyed the book that you told me to read it.

3. I still remember the man who he taught me to play the violin when I was a boy.

4. I showed my father a picture of the car I am going to buy it as soon as I save enough money.

5. The woman about who I was talking about suddenly walked into the room. I hope she didn't hear me.

6. Almost all of the people appear on television wear makeup.

7. My grandfather was a community leader whom everyone in our town admired him very much.

8. I don't like to spend time with people which loses their tempers easily.

9. I sit next to a person who his name is Ahmed.

10. In one corner of the marketplace, an old man who was playing a violin.

◇ **PRACTICE 9—SELFSTUDY: Adjective clauses: using *where* and *when*. (Charts 6-5 and 6-6)**

Directions: Combine the sentences by using either *where* or *when* to introduce an adjective clause.

1. That is the place. The accident occurred there.

  →*That is the place **where** the accident occurred.*

2. There was a time. Movies cost a dime then.

  →*There was a time **when** movies cost a dime.*

3. A cafe is a small restaurant. People can get a light meal there.

4. Every neighborhood in Brussels has small cafes. Customers drink coffee and eat pastries there.

5. There was a time. Dinosaurs dominated the earth then.

6. The house was destroyed in an earthquake ten years ago. I was born and grew up there.

7. Summer is the time of year. The weather is the hottest then.

8. The miser hid his money in a place. It was safe from robbers there.

9. There came a time. The miser had to spend his money then.

10. His new shirt didn't fit, so Dan took it back to the store. He'd bought it there.

◇ PRACTICE 10—GUIDED STUDY: Writing adjective clauses. (Charts 6-1 → 6-7)

Directions: Write sentences in which you use the given groups of words. Do not change the given words in any way. Each sentence should contain an adjective clause.

Examples:
the people I → *Most of **the people I** have met since I came here have been very friendly.*
the people that I → *One of **the people that I** admire most in the history of the world is Gandhi.*
the people with whom I → *I enjoyed talking to **the people with whom I** had dinner last night.*

1. the things I	7. the time my	13. everything you
2. the people who	8. a person whose	14. those who
3. a person who	9. a woman I	15. the only one who
4. the man to whom I	10. employees who	16. nothing I
5. the place I	11. the restaurant where	17. everyone she
6. a book that	12. someone that I	18. the doctor he

◇ PRACTICE 11—GUIDED STUDY: Writing. (Charts 6-1 → 6-7)

Directions: In writing, define a friend. What are the qualities you look for in a friend? What does a friend do or not do? Tell your reader about your friends. Who are they and what are they like?

◇ PRACTICE 12—SELFSTUDY: Punctuation of adjective clauses. (Chart 6-8)

Directions: Circle YES if the adjective clause requires commas and add the commas in the appropriate places. Circle NO if the adjective clause does not require commas.

1. YES (NO) The newspaper article was about a man who died two years ago of a rare tropical disease.

2. (YES) NO Paul O'Grady , who died two years ago , was a kind and loving man.

3. YES NO I made an appointment with a doctor who is considered an expert on eye disorders.

4. YES NO I made an appointment with Dr. Raven who is considered an expert on eye disorders.

5. YES NO The car that Al bought had had three previous owners, but it was in excellent condition.

6. YES NO We thoroughly enjoyed the music which we heard at the concert last Sunday.

7. YES NO Bogota which is the capital of Colombia is a cosmopolitan city.

8. YES NO They climbed Mount Rainier which is in the State of Washington twice last year.

9. YES NO Emeralds which are valuable gemstones are mined in Colombia.

10. YES NO The company offered the position to John whose department performed best this year.

11. YES NO On our trip to Africa, we visited Nairobi which is near several fascinating game reserves and then traveled to Egypt to see the pyramids.

12. YES NO I think the waiter who took our order used to work at Captain Bob's Restaurant.

13. YES NO Someone who understands physics better than I do is going to have to help you.

14. YES NO   Larry was very close to his only brother who was a famous social historian.

15. YES NO   Violent tropical storms that occur in western Asia are called typhoons.

16. YES NO   Similar storms that occur on the Atlantic side of the Americas are called hurricanes rather than typhoons.

17. YES NO   A typhoon which is a violent tropical storm can cause great destruction.

18. YES NO   According to the news report, the typhoon that threatened to strike the Indonesian coast has moved away from land and toward open water.

◇ PRACTICE 13—SELFSTUDY: Punctuation of adjective clauses. (Chart 6-8)

Directions: Choose the correct answer or answers.

1. Ms. Donaldson, _____**A**_____ teaches linguistics at the university, recently received recognition for her research on the use of gestures in communication.
   A. who   B. whom   C. which   D. that   E. ø

2. A woman _____**A, D**_____ teaches linguistics at the university received an award for outstanding research.
   A. who   B. whom   C. which   D. that   E. ø

3. The earth, _____ is the fifth largest planet in the solar system, is the third planet from the sun.
   A. who   B. whom   C. which   D. that   E. ø

4. A grant of $1.5 million was awarded to Dr. Sato, _____ has impressed the scientific community with his research on the common cold.
   A. who   B. whom   C. which   D. that   E. ø

5. The award for the Most Valuable Player was won by a player _____ the coaches and the entire team respect.
   A. who   B. whom   C. which   D. that   E. ø

6. The award was won by Dennis Johnson, _____ the coach highly respects.
   A. who   B. whom   C. which   D. that   E. ø

7. My accountant, _____ understands the complexities of the tax system, is doing my taxes this year.
   A. who   B. whom   C. which   D. that   E. ø

8. The school board voted to close a neighborhood elementary school. The decision, _____ affected over 200 students, was not warmly received in the community.
   A. who   B. whom   C. which   D. that   E. ø

9. Our office needs a secretary _____ knows how to use various word processing programs.
   A. who   B. whom   C. which   D. that   E. ø

10. The winner of the Nobel Prize in physics dedicated the honor to his high school physics teacher, _____ had been an inspiration during his early years.
    A. who   B. whom   C. which   D. that   E. ø

11. The consultant _____ was hired to advise us never really understood our situation.
    A. who   B. whom   C. which   D. that   E. ø

12. I gave the check to Oliver, _____ promptly cashed it and spent all the money before the day was out.
    A. who   B. whom   C. which   D. that   E. ø

13. The check _____ I gave to Oliver was for work he'd done for me.
    A. who   B. whom   C. which   D. that   E. ø

Directions: Choose the correct explanation of the meaning of each sentence.

1. The students, who attend class five hours per day, have become quite proficient in their new language.
   - (a.) *All* of the students attend class for five hours per day.
   - b. *Only some* of the students attend class for five hours per day.

2. The students who attend class five hours per day have become quite proficient in their new language.
   - a. *All* of the students attend class for five hours per day.
   - (b.) *Only some* of the students attend class for five hours per day.

3. The orchestra conductor signaled the violinists, who were to begin playing.
   - a. *All* of the violinists were to begin playing.
   - b. *Only some* of the violinists were to begin playing.

4. The orchestra conductor signaled the violinists who were to begin playing.
   - a. *All* of the violinists were to begin playing.
   - b. *Only some* of the violinists were to begin playing.

5. I put the vase on top of the TV set, which is in the living room.
   - a. I have *more than one* TV set.
   - b. I have *only one* TV set.

6. I put the vase on top of the TV set that is in the living room.
   - a. I have *more than one* TV set.
   - b. I have *only one* TV set.

7. Trees which lose their leaves in winter are called deciduous trees.
   - a. *All* trees lose their leaves in winter.
   - b. *Only some* trees lose their leaves in winter.

8. Pine trees, which are evergreen, grow well in a cold climate.
   - a. *All* pine trees are evergreen.
   - b. *Only some* pine trees are evergreen.

◇ PRACTICE 15—SELFSTUDY: Punctuation of adjective clauses. (Charts 6-8 → 6-11)

Directions: Circle YES if the adjective clause requires commas and add the commas in the appropriate places. Circle NO if the adjective clause does not require commas.

1. (YES) NO Thirty people **,** two of whom were members of the crew **,** were killed in the ferry accident.

2. YES (NO) I'm trying to convince my mother to buy a small car which has front-wheel drive instead of a large car with rear-wheel drive.

3. YES NO Over 500 students took the entrance examination the results of which will be posted in the administration building at the end of the month.

4. YES NO   The newspapers carried the story of an accident in which four pedestrians were injured.
5. YES NO   The newly married couple that lives next door just moved here from California.
6. YES NO   The Caspian Sea which is bounded by the Soviet Union and Iran is fed by eight rivers.
7. YES NO   The new supervisor was not happy with his work crew none of whom seemed interested in doing quality work.
8. YES NO   My oldest brother in whose house I lived for six months when I was ten has been a father to me in many ways.
9. YES NO   Tom is always interrupting me which makes me mad.
10. YES NO   To express the uselessness of worrying, Mark Twain once said, ''I've had a lot of problems in my life most of which never happened.''

◇ **PRACTICE 16—SELFSTUDY: Expressions of quantity in adjective clauses. (Chart 6-9)**

Directions: Combine the sentences. Use the second sentence as an adjective clause.

1. I received two job offers. I accepted neither of them.
   → *I received two job offers, neither of which I accepted.*

2. I have three brothers. Two of them are professional athletes.
3. Jerry is engaged in several business ventures. Only one of them is profitable.
4. The United States of America is a union of fifty states. The majority of them are located east of the Mississippi River.
5. The two women have already dissolved their business partnership. Both of them are changing careers.
6. Tom is proud of his success. Much of it has been due to hard work, but some of it has been due to good luck.

◇ **PRACTICE 17—SELFSTUDY: Using *which* to modify a sentence. (Chart 6-11)**

Directions: Combine the sentences, using *which*.

1. Sally lost her job. That wasn't surprising.
   → *Sally lost her job, which wasn't surprising.*

2. She usually came to work late. That upset her boss.
3. So her boss fired her. That made her angry.
4. She hadn't saved any money. That was unfortunate.
5. So she had to borrow some money from me. I didn't like that.
6. She has found a new job. That is lucky.
7. So she has repaid the money she borrowed from me. I appreciate that.
8. She has promised herself to be on time to work every day. That is a good idea.

◇ PRACTICE 18—GUIDED STUDY: Special adjective clauses. (Charts 6-9 → 6-11)

Directions: Write sentences that contain the following groups of words. Do not change the order of the words as they are given. Add words only before and/or after the group of words. Add punctuation as necessary.

Examples:

   . . . yesterday which surprised. . . .
   → *Tom didn't come to class **yesterday, which surprised** me.*

   . . . people to my party some of whom. . . .
   → *I invited ten **people to my party, some of whom** are my classmates.*

1. . . . brothers all of whom . . .
2. . . . early which was fortunate . . .
3. . . . students three of whom . . .
4. . . . ideas none of which . . .
5. . . . jewelry the value of which . . .
6. . . . teachers some of whom . . .
7. . . . mother which made me . . .
8. . . . a little money all of which . . .
9. . . . sisters each of whom . . .
10. . . . new car the inside of which . . .
11. . . . clothes some of which . . .
12. . . . yesterday which surprised . . .

◇ PRACTICE 19—GUIDED STUDY: Writing adjective clauses. (Charts 6-1 → 6-11)

Directions: Combine the sentences. Use (b) as an adjective clause. Punctuate carefully. Use formal written English.

1. (a) The blue whale is considered the largest animal that has ever lived.
   (b) It can grow to 100 feet and 150 tons.
   → *The blue whale, which can grow to 100 feet and 150 tons, is considered the largest animal that has ever lived.*

2. (a) An antecedent is a word.
   (b) A pronoun refers to this word.
   → *An antecedent is a word to which a pronoun refers.*

3. (a) The plane was met by a crowd of three hundred people.
   (b) Some of them had been waiting for more than four hours.

4. (a) In this paper, I will describe the basic process.
   (b) Raw cotton becomes cotton thread by this process.

5. (a) The researchers are doing case studies of people to determine the importance of heredity in health and longevity.
   (b) These people's families have a history of high blood pressure and heart disease.

6. (a) At the end of this month, scientists at the institute will conclude their AIDS* research.
   (b) The results of this research will be published within six months.

7. (a) People may become anxious and worried.
   (b) They are forced to retire in their middle or late sixties.

8. (a) My parents look forward to retirement.
   (b) They know how to enjoy themselves and their family.

_____

*AIDS = **A**cquired **I**mmune **D**eficiency **S**yndrome

9. (a) According to many education officials, "math phobia" (that is, a fear of mathematics) is a widespread problem.
    (b) A solution to this problem must and can be found.

10. (a) The art museum hopes to hire a new administrator.
    (b) Under this person's direction it will be able to purchase significant pieces of art.

11. (a) The giant anteater licks up ants for its dinner.
    (b) Its tongue is longer than 30 centimeters (12 inches).

12. (a) The anteater's tongue is sticky.
    (b) It can go in and out of its mouth 160 times a minute.

◇ **PRACTICE 20—SELFSTUDY: Adjective phrases. (Charts 6-12 and 6-13)**

Directions: Change the adjective clauses to adjective phrases.

1. Only a few of the movies that are shown at the Gray Theater are suitable for children.
   → *Only a few of the movies shown at the Gray Theater are suitable for children.*

2. Jasmine, which is a viny plant with fragrant flowers, grows only in warm places.
   → *Jasmine, a viny plant with fragrant flowers, grows only in warm places.*

3. The couple who live in the house next door are both college professors.
   → *The couple living in the house next door are both college professors.*

4. A throne is the chair which is occupied by a queen, king, or other rulers.

5. A knuckle is a joint that connects a finger to the rest of the hand.

6. We visited Belgrade, which is the capital city of Yugoslavia.

7. Antarctica is covered by a huge ice cap that contains 70 percent of the earth's fresh water.

8. Astronomy, which is the study of planets and stars, is one of the world's oldest sciences.

9. Only a small fraction of the eggs that are laid by a fish actually hatch and survive to adulthood.

10. Our solar system is in a galaxy that is called the Milky Way.

11. Two out of three people who are struck by lightning survive.

12. Arizona, which was once thought to be a useless desert, is today a rapidly growing industrial and agricultural state.

13. Simon Bolivar, who was a great South American general, led the fight for independence in the early 19th century.

14. In hot weather, many people enjoy lemonade, which is a drink that is made of lemon juice, water, and sugar.

15. I was awakened by the sound of laughter which came from the room which was next door to mine at the motel.

16. Few tourists ever see a jaguar, which is a spotted wild cat that is native to tropical America.

◇ PRACTICE 21—SELFSTUDY: Punctuation of adjective phrases. (Charts 6-12 and 6-13)

Directions: Add commas where necessary.

1. A national holiday has been established in memory of Martin Luther King, Jr., the leader of the civil rights movement in the United States in the 1950s and 1960s.

2. Neil Armstrong the first person to set foot on the moon reported that the surface was fine and powdery.

3. Susan B. Anthony the first and only woman whose picture appears on U. S. money worked tirelessly during her lifetime to gain the right to vote for women.

4. Mark Twain is an author known far and wide as one of the greatest American humorists.

5. Many famous people did not enjoy immediate success in their lives. Abraham Lincoln one of the truly great presidents of the United States ran for public office 26 times and lost 23 of the elections. Walt Disney the creator of Mickey Mouse and founder of his own movie production company once got fired by a newspaper editor because he had no good ideas. Thomas Edison the inventor of the light bulb and phonograph was believed by his teachers to be too stupid to learn. Albert Einstein one of the greatest scientists of all time performed badly in almost all of his high school courses and failed his college entrance exam.

◇ PRACTICE 22—SELFSTUDY: Adjective phrases. (Charts 6-12 and 6-13)

Directions: Complete the sentences in *PART II* with adjective phrases by using the information in *PART I*. Use commas as necessary.

PART I:
  A. It is the lowest place on the earth's surface.
✔ B. It is the highest mountain in the world.
  C. It is the capital of Iraq.
  D. It is the capital of Argentina.
  E. It is the largest city in the western hemisphere.
  F. It is the largest city in the United States.
  G. It is the most populous country in Africa.
  H. It is the northernmost country in Latin America.
  I. It is an African animal that eats ants and termites.
  J. It is a small animal that spends its entire life underground.
  K. They are sensitive instruments that measure the shaking of the ground.
  L. They are devices that produce a powerful beam of light.

PART II:

1. Mt. Everest _____ **the highest mountain in the world,** _____ is in the Himalayas.

2. One of the largest cities in the Middle East is Baghdad _____.

3. Earthquakes are recorded on seismographs _____.

4. The Dead Sea _____ is located in the Middle East between Jordan and Israel.

5. The newspaper reported a minor earthquake in Buenos Aires _____.

6. Industry and medicine are continually finding new uses for lasers _____.

7. Mexico _____ lies just south of the United States.

8. Even though the nation consists of more than 250 different cultural groups, English is the official language of Nigeria _____.

9. Both Mexico City _____ and New York City _____ face challenging futures.

10. The mole _____ is almost blind. The aardvark _____ also lives underground but hunts for its food above ground.

◇ **PRACTICE 23—GUIDED STUDY: Adjective phrases. (Charts 6-12 and 6-13)**

Directions: Change all of the adjective clauses to adjective phrases.

1. None of the pedestrians who were walking up and down the busy street stopped to help or even inquire about the elderly man who was slumped in the doorway of an apparently unoccupied building.
   → *None of the pedestrians walking up and down the busy street stopped to help or even inquire about the elderly man slumped in the doorway of an apparently unoccupied building.*

2. Food that passes from the mouth to the stomach goes through a tube which is called the esophagus.

3. Animals that are born in a zoo generally adjust to captivity better than those that are captured in the wild.

4. The children attended a special movie program that consisted of cartoons that featured Donald Duck and Mickey Mouse.

5. One of the most important foodstuffs in the world is flour, which is a fine powder that is made by grinding wheat or other grains.

6. My uncle Elias, who is a restaurant owner, often buys fish and shellfish from boats that are docked at the local pier. Customers come from miles around to dine on a seafood feast that is considered to be the best in all of the northeastern United States.

7. Hundreds of volunteers went to a northern village yesterday to reinforce firefighters who are trying to save a settlement which is threatened by a forest fire. The fire started when a cigarette ignited oil which was leaking from a machine which is used to cut timber.

8. Researchers have developed a way to mark genes so that they glow in the dark, which is a technique that scientists can use to follow specific genetic activity of cells which are within plants and animals. This development, which was announced by the National Science Foundation, which is the sponsor of the research, should prove useful to scientists who study the basic functions of organisms.

9. A discovery and an invention are different, but they are related. A discovery occurs when something that exists in nature is recognized for the first time. Fire is an example of a discovery. An invention is something that is made for the first time by a creator. An invention never existed before the act of creation. The telephone and the automobile, which are two examples of important twentieth century inventions, illustrate the way in which inventions give people control over their environment and enable them to live better lives.

◇ **PRACTICE 24—GUIDED STUDY: Speaking and writing. (Chapter 6)**

Directions: Either in a group or by yourself, draw up a list of inventions made in the 20th century. Discuss the inventions you have named, using the following questions as guidelines:

1. What are the three most important twentieth century inventions that you have listed? Why? In other words, why do you rate these as the most influential/important inventions?
2. What were important inventions prior to the twentieth century? Why?
3. Which invention has brought the most happiness to people? Which has caused the most unhappiness?
4. Are any of the inventions you have listed luxury items? Which of the inventions you have listed have become accepted as necessities?
5. What would your world be like without a certain invention? How has your life been influenced by these inventions? Would you like to go back to 1900 when none of these things existed? Can you visualize life as it was then?
6. What would you like to see invented now? What do you think will be one of the most important inventions that will be made in the future? What are you going to invent?

◇ **PRACTICE 25—GUIDED STUDY: Adjective clauses and phrases. (Charts 6-2 → 6-13)**

Directions: Combine each group of short, choppy sentences into one sentence. Use the underlined sentence as the independent clause; build your sentence around the independent clause. Use adjective clauses and adjective phrases wherever possible.

1. Chihuahua is divided into two regions. It is the largest Mexican state. One region is a mountainous area in the west. The other region is a desert basin in the north and east.
   → *Chihuahua*, *the largest Mexican state*, *is divided into two regions*, *a mountainous area in the west and a desert basin in the north and east.*

2. Disney World covers a large area of land. It is an amusement park. It is located in Orlando, Florida. The land includes lakes, golf courses, campsites, hotels, and a wildlife preserve.

3. Jamaica is one of the world's leading producers of bauxite. It is the third largest island in the Caribbean Sea. Bauxite is an ore. Aluminum is made from this ore.

4. Robert Ballard made headlines in 1985. He is an oceanographer. In 1985 he discovered the remains of the Titanic. The Titanic was the "unsinkable" passenger ship. It has rested on the floor of the Atlantic Ocean since 1912. It struck an iceberg in 1912 and sank.

5. William Shakespeare's father was a glove maker and a town official. William Shakespeare's father was John Shakespeare. He owned a shop in Stratford-upon-Avon. Stratford-upon-Avon is a town. It is about 75 miles (120 kilometers) northwest of London.

6. The Yemen Arab Republic is an ancient land. It is located at the southwestern tip of the Arabian Peninsula. This land has been host to many prosperous civilizations. These civilizations include the Kingdom of Sheba and various Islamic empires.

◇ **PRACTICE 26—SELFSTUDY: Error analysis. (Charts 6-2 → 6-13)**

Directions: All of the following sentences contain errors in adjective clauses, adjective phrases, or punctuation. Find the errors and correct them, using any appropriate form.

1. One of the people which I admire most is my uncle.

2. Baseball is the only sport in which I am interested in it.

3. My favorite teacher, Mr. Peterson, he was always willing to help me after class.

4. There are some people in the government who is trying to improve the lives of poor people.

5. I have some good advice for anyone who he wants to learn a second language.

6. My classroom is located on the second floor of Carver Hall that is a large brick building in the center of the campus.

7. When we walked past the theater, there were a lot of people waited in a long line outside the box office.

8. Students who living on campus are close to their classrooms and the library.

9. A myth is a story expresses traditional beliefs.

10. If you need any information, see the librarian sits at the central desk on the second floor.

11. My oldest sister is Anna is 21 years old.

12. Hiroko was born in Sapporo that is a city in Japan.

13. Patrick who is my oldest brother. He is married and has one child.

14. The person sits next to me is someone I've never met him.

15. My favorite place in the world is a small city is located on the southern coast of Brazil.

◇ **PRACTICE 27—GUIDED STUDY: Error analysis. (Chapter 6)**

Directions: All of the following sentences contain errors in adjective clauses, adjective phrases, or punctuation. Find the errors and correct them, using any appropriate form.

1. Last Saturday I attended a party giving by one of my friends. My friend, who his apartment is in another town, was very glad that I could come.

2. Dr. Darnell was the only person to whom I wanted to see.

3. There are eighty students, are from all over the world, study English at this school.

4. The people who we met them on our trip last May are going to visit us in October.

5. Dianne Jones that used to teach Spanish has organized a tour of Central America for senior citizens.

6. There is an old legend telling among people in my country about a man lived in the seventeenth century saved a village from destruction.

7. I've met many people since I came here who some of them are from my country.

8. An old man was fishing next to me on the pier was muttering to himself.

9. People can speak English can be understood in many countries.

10. When I was a child, I was always afraid of the beggars whom they went from house to house in my neighborhood.

11. At the national park, there is a path leads to a spectacular waterfall.

12. The road that we took it through the forest it was narrow and steep.

◇ **PRACTICE 28—GUIDED STUDY. Writing game. (Chapter 6)**

Directions: Form a group of three people. Together, make up one sentence with as many adjective clauses as possible. In other words, make the most awkward sentence you can while still using grammatically correct sentence structure. Count the number of adjective clauses you use. See which group can make the worst sentence by using the largest number of adjective clauses.

Example of a stylistically terrible, but grammatically correct, sentence:
The man who was sitting at a table which was at the restaurant where I usually eat dinner, which is something I do every evening, was talking to a woman who was wearing a dress which was blue, which is my favorite color.

◇ **PRACTICE 29—GUIDED STUDY. Writing. (Chapter 6)**

Directions: Write on one, two, or all of the following topics. Try to use adjective clauses and phrases as appropriate.

1. Write about three historical figures from your country. Give your reader information about their lives and accomplishments.
2. Write about your favorite TV shows. What are they? What are they about? Why do you enjoy them?
3. Who are some people in your country who are popular with young people (e.g., singers, movie stars, political figures, etc.)? Tell your readers about these people. Assume your readers are completely unfamiliar with them.
4. You are a tourist agent for your hometown/country. Write a descriptive brochure that would make your reader want to visit your hometown/country.
5. What kind of people do you like? What kind of people do you avoid?
6. What kind of person do you want to marry? What kind of person do you not want to marry? If you are already married, what kind of person did you marry?

◇ **PRACTICE TEST A—SELFSTUDY: Adjective clauses. (Chapter 6)**

Directions: Choose the correct answer.

Example:
Friends are people __**B**__ *close to us.*
    A. *who is*   B. *who are*   C. *which is*   D. *which are*

1. "Who is eligible for the scholarship?"
   "Anyone _____ scholastic record is above average can apply for the scholarship."
      A. who has a   B. has a   C. who's a   D. whose

2. Dr. Sales is a person _____.
      A. in whom I don't have much confidence   B. in that I don't have much confidence
      C. whom I don't have much confidence in him   D. I don't have much confidence

3. "Is April twenty-first the day _____?"
   "No, the twenty-second."
      A. you'll arrive then   B. when you'll arrive
      C. on that you'll arrive   D. when you'll arrive on

4. The severe drought _____ occurred last summer ruined the corn crop.
   A. that it   B. which it   C. it   D. that

5. Florida, _____ the Sunshine State, attracts many tourists every year.
   A. is   B. known as   C. is known as   D. that is known as

6. The new shopping mall is gigantic. It's advertised as a place _____ you can find just about anything you might want to buy.
   A. where   B. which   C. in where   D. in that

7. Lola's marriage has been arranged by her family. She is marrying a man _____.
   A. that she hardly knows him   B. whom she hardly knows him
   C. she hardly knows   D. she hardly knows him

8. People who exercise frequently have greater physical endurance than those _____.
   A. who doesn't   B. that doesn't   C. which don't   D. who don't

9. "Is this the address to _____ you want the package sent?"
   "Yes."
   A. where   B. that   C. which   D. whom

10. Ann quit her job at the advertising agency, _____ surprised everyone.
    A. which   B. that   C. who   D. that it

11. That book is by a famous anthropologist. It's about the people in Samoa _____ for two years.
    A. that she lived   B. that she lived among them
    C. among whom she lived   D. where she lived among them

12. The missing man's family is desperately seeking anyone _____ information about his activities or whereabouts.
    A. has   B. having   C. who have   D. have

13. The publishers expect that the new biography of Simon Bolivar will be bought by people _____ in Latin American history.
    A. who they are interested   B. are interested
    C. interested   D. they are interested

14. I have always wanted to visit Paris, _____ of France.
    A. is the capital   B. which the capital is
    C. that is the capital   D. the capital

15. The chemistry book _____ was a little expensive.
    A. that I bought it   B. I bought that   C. what I bought   D. I bought

16. "Have you ever met the man _____ over there?"
    "No. Who is he?"
    A. stands   B. standing
    C. is standing   D. who he is standing

17. "Do you have the book _____ the teacher?"
    "Yes, I do."
    A. that it belongs to   B. to which belongs to
    C. to which belongs   D. that belongs to

18. The voters were overwhelmingly against the candidate _____ proposals called for higher taxes.
    A. who his   B. whose   C. whom he had   D. that his

19. "Do you remember Mrs. Goddard, _____ taught us English composition?"
    "I certainly do."
    A. who   B. whom   C. that   D. which

20. I have three brothers, _____ are businessmen.
    A. that all of them   B. who they all   C. all of whom   D. who all of them

Directions: Choose the correct answer.

Example:
Friends are people __**B**__ *close to us.*
    A. who is   *B. who are*   *C. which is*   *D. which are*

1. "Were you able to locate the person _____ wallet you found?"
   "Luckily, yes."
       A. which   B. that his   C. whose   D. that's

2. Some fish is frozen, but _____ is best.
       A. fish is fresh   B. fresh fish
       C. fish fresh   D. fresh fish is caught

3. "Why do you get up at 4:00 A.M.?"
   "Because it's the only time _____ without being interrupted."
       A. when I can work on my book   B. when I can work on my book at
       C. when I can work on my book then   D. at when I can work on my book

4. "You seem so happy today."
   "I am. You are looking at a person _____ has just been accepted into medical school!"
       A. who   B. who she   C. whom she   D. whom

5. "The movie _____ last night was terrific."
   "What's it about?"
       A. I went   B. I went to it   C. I went to   D. that I went

6. Many people lost their homes in the earthquake. The government needs to establish more shelters to care for those _____ have homes.
       A. who doesn't   B. who don't   C. which doesn't   D. which don't

7. The problem _____ never occurred.
       A. I had expected it   B. who I had expected
       C. that I had expected it   D. I had expected

8. I had to drive to the factory to pick up my brother, _____ car wouldn't start.
       A. who his   B. who   C. who's   D. whose

9. I read a book about Picasso, _____ .
       A. is a Spanish painter   B. a Spanish painter
       C. who a Spanish painter is   D. that is a Spanish painter

10. The people _____ the acrobat turn circles in the air were horrified when he missed the outstretched hands of his partner and fell to his death.
        A. watched   B. watch   C. watching   D. were watching

11. "My writing has improved a lot in this class."
    "Mine has, too. All the students _____ do well in writing."
        A. whom Mr. Davis teaches them   B. which Mr. Davis teaches
        C. that Mr. Davis teaches them   D. Mr. Davis teaches

12. "Have you seen the place _____ the graduation ceremony will be held?"
    "Yes. It's big enough to hold 5,000 people."
        A. in that   B. where   C. is where that   D. which

13. "How's your class this term?"
    "Great. I have seventeen students, most of _____ speak English very well."
        A. who   B. those   C. whom   D. which

14. "Will everyone like the book?"
    "No. Only people _____ interested in anthropology."
        A. are   B. who are   C. in whom are   D. that is

15. "How did you enjoy your dinner with Mr. Jackson?"
    "It was boring. He talked only about himself, _____ almost put us to sleep."
       A. which   B. that   C. who   D. that he

16. My grandfather, _____ a wise man, has greatly influenced my life.
       A. is   B. that is   C. who is   D. who he is

17. "Is Dr. Brown the person _____ you wish to speak?"
    "Yes, please."
       A. that   B. whom   C. to that   D. to whom

18. In the movie, a teenager _____ to pursue a singing career meets resistance from his strong-willed father.
       A. wants   B. wanted   C. wanting   D. who want

19. "Excuse me, but there is something about _____ immediately."
    "Certainly."
       A. which I must speak to you   B. which I must speak to you about it
       C. that I must speak to you about   D. that I must speak to you

20. *Little Women*, _____ in 1868, is my sister's favorite book.
       A. is a novel published   B. a novel published
       C. a novel was published   D. was a novel published

CHAPTER 7
Noun Clauses

◇ **PRACTICE 1—SELFSTUDY:** Questions and noun clauses that begin with a question word. (Charts 7-1 and 7-2; Appendix 1, B-1 and B-2)

Directions: Look at the <u>underlined</u> part of each sentence. If the underlined part is a question, circle **Q.** If it is a noun clause, circle **N.Cl.** Then add the necessary final punctuation: a period (.) or a question mark (?).

1. (**Q**)**N.Cl.**   I couldn't hear him. <u>What did he say</u>**?**
2. **Q** (**N.Cl.**)   I couldn't hear <u>what he said</u>**.**
3. **Q N.Cl.**   I need some information. <u>Where does Tom live</u>   I have to send him a letter.
4. **Q N.Cl.**   I need to know <u>where Tom lives</u>   I have to send him a letter.
5. **Q N.Cl.**   There's something I don't understand. <u>Why did Barb cancel her vacation plans</u>
6. **Q N.Cl.**   I don't understand <u>why Barb canceled her vacation plans</u>
7. **Q N.Cl.**   I can't tell you <u>what they did</u>   You'll have to ask Jim.
8. **Q N.Cl.**   <u>What did they do</u>   Please tell me.
9. **Q N.Cl.**   Do you know that woman? <u>Who is she</u>   She looks familiar.
10. **Q N.Cl.**   Do you see that woman over there? Do you know <u>who she is</u>   She looks familiar.
11. **Q N.Cl.**   <u>Where did Ann go</u>   Do you know?
12. **Q N.Cl.**   <u>Where Ann went</u>   is a secret

◇ **PRACTICE 2—SELFSTUDY:** Questions and noun clauses that begin with a question word. (Charts 7-1 and 7-2; Appendix 1, B-1 and B-2)

Directions: If the given words are a question, insert a capital letter and a question mark. If the given words are a noun clause, write *"I don't know"* and a final period.

1. _____**W** ⁄where is he **?**_____
2. _**I don't know** where he is.__
3. _**I don't know** what he did.__
4. _____**W** ⁄what did he do **?**_____
5. _____ how old is he
6. _____ how old he is
7. _____ where did he go
8. _____ where he went
9. _____ why he said that
10. _____ why did he say that
11. _____ who he is
12. _____ who is he
13. _____ when will he arrive
14. _____ when he will arrive
15. _____ who is he talking to
16. _____ which one he bought

◇ **PRACTICE 3—SELFSTUDY:** Forms of information questions and noun clauses.
(Charts 7-1 and 7-2; Appendix 1, Charts B-1 and B-2)

Directions: Make a question from the given sentence. The words in parentheses should be the answer to the question you make. Use a question word (*who, what, how, etc.*). Then change the question to a noun clause.

1. Tom will be here (*next week*).

    QUESTION: _____*When will Tom be here?*_____

    NOUN CLAUSE: Please tell me _____*when Tom will be here.*_____

2. He is coming (*because he wants to visit his friends*).

    QUESTION: _____

    NOUN CLAUSE: Please tell me _____

3. He'll be on flight (*645, not flight 742*).

    QUESTION: _____

    NOUN CLAUSE: Please tell me _____

4. (*Jim Hunter*) is going to meet him at the airport.

    QUESTION: _____

    NOUN CLAUSE: Please tell me _____

5. Jim Hunter is (*his roommate*).

    QUESTION: _____

    NOUN CLAUSE: Please tell me _____

6. Tom's address is (*4149 Riverside Road*).

    QUESTION: _____

    NOUN CLAUSE: Please tell me _____

7. He lives (*on Riverside Road in Columbus, Ohio, USA*).

    QUESTION: _____

    NOUN CLAUSE: Please tell me _____

8. He was (*in Chicago*) last week.

    QUESTION: _____

    NOUN CLAUSE: Please tell me _____

9. He has been working for IBM★ (*since 1988*).

    QUESTION: _____

    NOUN CLAUSE: Do you know _____

10. He has (*an IBM*) computer at home.

    QUESTION: _____

    NOUN CLAUSE: Do you know _____

_____
★IBM = the name of a corporation (**I**nternational **B**usiness **M**achines)

11. He needs (*some new disks for his computer*).

QUESTION: _____

NOUN CLAUSE: Do you know _____

12. He called (*yesterday*).

QUESTION: _____

NOUN CLAUSE: Please tell me _____

13. He wants to (*see all his friends*) after he gets here.

QUESTION: _____

NOUN CLAUSE: Do you know _____

14. It was (*his*) idea to have a party.

QUESTION: _____

NOUN CLAUSE: Can you tell me _____

◇ **PRACTICE 4—SELFSTUDY: Questions and noun clauses that begin with a question word.**
(Charts 7-1 and 7-2; Appendix 1, B-1 and B-2)

Directions: Use the words in parentheses to complete the sentences. Use any appropriate verb tense. Some of the completions contain noun clauses and some contain questions.

1. A: Where _____*did Ruth go*_____? She's not in her room. (*Ruth, go*)

   B: I don't know. Ask Tina. She might know where _____*Ruth went*_____. (*Ruth, go*)

2. A: John is searching every drawer. Do you know what _____*he's looking for*_____? (*he, look for*)

   B: I have no idea. Why don't I just ask him? John? What _____*are you looking for*_____? (*you, look for*)

3. A: Oops! I made a mistake. Where _____? Didn't I lend it to you? (*my eraser, be*)

   B: I don't have it. Ask Sally where _____. I think I saw her using it. (*it, be*)

4. A: I heard that Sam changed his mind about going on the picnic. Why _____ to stay home? Is something wrong? (*he, decide*)

   B: I don't know. Maybe Jane can tell us why _____ not to come with us. Let's ask her. I hope he's okay. (*he, decide*)

5. A: Whose book _____? (*this, be*)

   B: It's not mine. I don't know whose _____. (*it, be*)

6. A: Did Jack get enough food when he went to the market? How much fish _____? It takes a lot of fish to feed 12 people. (*he, buy*)

   B: Just relax. I don't know exactly how much fish _____, but I'm sure there'll be enough for dinner for all of us. (*he, buy*)

7. A: The door isn't locked! Why _____ it before he left? (*Fred, lock,*
      not)

   B: Why ask me? How am I supposed to know why _____ it?
      Maybe he just forgot. (*he, lock, not*)

8. A: The Lee family are recent immigrants, aren't they? How long _____
      in this country? (*they, be*)

   B: I have no idea. Would you like me to ask Mr. Lee how long _____
      _____ here? I'll be seeing him this afternoon. (*he and his family, live*)

9. A: I need a math tutor. Do you know who _____? (*John's tutor, be*)

   B: No. Let me ask Phil. Excuse me, Phil? Who _____? Do you
      know? (*John's tutor, be*)

10. A: You're a student here? I'm a student here, too. Tell me what classes _____
       _____ this term. Maybe we're in some of the same classes. (*you, take*)

    B: Math 4, English 2, History 6, and Chemistry 101. What classes _____
       _____? (*you, take*)

11. A: Lucy, why _____ for the exam? You could have done much
       better if you'd been prepared. (*you, study, not*)

    B: Well, Professor Morris, why _____ for the exam is a long story.
       I intended to, but . . . . (*I, study, not*)

12. A: Help! Quick! Look at that road sign! Which road _____ to
       take? (*we, be supposed*)

    B: You're the driver! Don't look at me! I don't know which road _____
       to take. I've never been here before in my entire life. (*we, be supposed*)

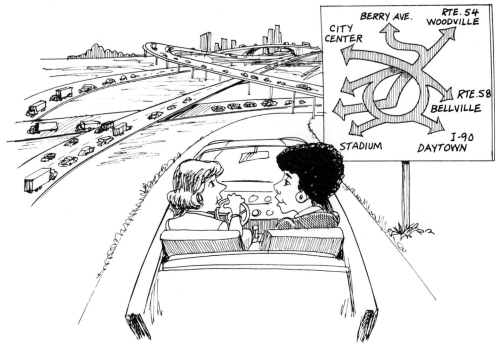

◇ **PRACTICE 5—GUIDED STUDY: Information questions and noun clauses.**
(Charts 7-2 and 7-3)

Directions: Pair up with another student.
  STUDENT A: Ask any question using the given words.
  STUDENT B: To make sure you understood Student A correctly, repeat what s/he said using a noun clause. Begin by saying: "You want to know . . . ."
Listen to each other's grammar carefully, especially word order.

Examples:

who/roommate	STUDENT A: *Who is your roommate?*
	STUDENT B: *You want to know who my roommate is.*
where/go	STUDENT A: *Where did you go after class yesterday?*
	STUDENT B: *You want to know where I went after class yesterday.*
how far/it	STUDENT A: *How far is it from Bangkok to Rangoon?*
	STUDENT B: *You want to know how far it is from Bangkok to Rangoon.*

PART I: (Appoint one of yourselves A and the other B.)

1. whose/that
2. how much/cost
3. what time/get
4. how long/you
5. what kind/have

6. when/you
7. where/last night
8. why/didn't
9. what/like
10. where/the teacher

11. who/prime minister
12. which/want
13. why/blue
14. what/after
15. from whom/borrow

PART II: (Switch roles: now B becomes A and asks the questions.)

1. where/born
2. what color/eyes
3. whose/is
4. which/you
5. why/ask

6. when/get
7. where/located
8. who/is
9. who/talk
10. how many/go

11. what/tomorrow
12. how far/it
13. what kind/buy
14. how often/you
15. to whom/give

◇ **PRACTICE 6—SELFSTUDY: Changing yes/no and information questions to noun clauses.**
(Charts 7-2 and 7-3)

Directions: Complete the sentence by changing the question in parentheses to a noun clause.

1. (*Will it rain?*) I wonder _____*if/whether it will rain*_____.

2. (*When will it rain?*) I wonder _____*when it will rain*_____.

3. (*Is Sam at home?*)

   I don't know _____ at home.

4. (*Where is Sam?*)

   I don't know _____.

5. (*Did Jane call?*)

   Ask Tom _____.

6. (*What time did she call?*)

   Ask Tom _____.

7. (*Why is the earth called "the water planet"?*)

   Do you know _____ "the water planet"?

8. (*How far is it from New York City to Jakarta?*)

   I wonder _____ from New York to Jakarta.

9. (*Has Susan ever been in Portugal?*)

   I wonder _____ in Portugal.

10. (*Does she speak Portuguese?*)

    I wonder _____ Portuguese.

11. (*Who did Ann play tennis with?*)

    I wonder _____ tennis with.

12. (*Who won the tennis match?*)

    I wonder _____ the tennis match.

13. (*Did Ann win?*)

    I wonder _____.

14. (*Do all creatures, including fish and insects, feel pain in the same way as humans do?*)

    I wonder _____ pain in the same way as humans do.

15. (*Can birds communicate with each other?*)

    Do you know _____ with each other?

16. (*How do birds communicate with each other?*)

Have you ever studied _____ with each other?

17. (*Where is the nearest post office?*)

Do you know _____?

18. (*Is there a post office near here?*)

Do you know _____ near here?

◇ **PRACTICE 7—SELFSTUDY: Error analysis. (Charts 7-2 and 7-3)**

Directions: Find and correct the errors in the following sentences.

1. Please tell me what is your name. → *Please tell me what **your name is**.*

2. No one seems to know when will Maria arrive.

3. I wonder why was Bob late for class.

4. I don't know what does that word mean.

5. I wonder does the teacher know the answer?

6. What should they do about the hole in their roof is their most pressing problem.

7. I'll ask her would she like some coffee or not.

8. Be sure to tell the doctor where does it hurt.

9. Why am I unhappy is something I can't explain.

10. I wonder does Tom know about the meeting or not.

11. I need to know who is your teacher.

12. I don't understand why is the car not running properly.

◇ **PRACTICE 8—SELFSTUDY: Question words and *whether* followed by infinitives. (Chart 7-4)**

Directions: Using the idea in the question in parentheses, complete the sentence with a question word or *whether* followed by an infinitive.

1. (*Where should I buy the meat for the lamb stew?*)

I don't know ___**where to buy**___ the meat for the lamb stew.

2. (*Should I stay home or go to the movie?*)

Tom can't decide ___**whether to stay**___ home or ___**go**___ to the movie.

3. (*How can I fix this toaster?*)

Jack doesn't know ___**how to fix**___ the toaster.

4. (*Should I look for another job?*)

Jason is wondering ___**whether (or not) to look**___ for another job.

5. (*Where can I get a map of the city?*)

Ann wants to know _____ a map of the city.

6. (*Should I go to the meeting?*)

Al is trying to decide _____ to the meeting.

7. (*What time should I pick you up?*)

I need to know _____ you up.

8. (*Who should I talk to about this problem?*)

I don't know _____ to about this problem.

9. (*Should I take a nap or do my homework?*)

I can't decide _____ a nap or _____ my homework.

10. (*How can I solve this problem for you?*)

My adviser can't figure out _____ this problem for me.

11. (*Where should I tell them to meet us?*)

I'm not sure _____ them to meet us.

12. (*How long am I supposed to cook this meat?*)

I can't remember _____ this meat.

13. (*What should I wear to the ceremony?*)

I can't decide _____ to the ceremony.

14. (*How much coffee should I make for the meeting?*)

You'll have to tell me _____ for the meeting.

15. (*Which essay should I use for the contest?*)

Susan can't decide _____ for the contest.

16. (*Should I take a year off from work and travel around the world? Or should I keep working and save my money?*)

Alice can't decide _____ a year off from work and _____ around the world, or _____ working and _____ her money.

◇ **PRACTICE 9—GUIDED STUDY:** *"That* clauses." (Chart 7-5)

Directions: Complete the sentences with your own words.

Examples:

    It is apparent that . . . .

    → *It is apparent that the weather is not going to improve.*

    That . . . is a fact that is hard to deny.

    → *That pollution diminishes the quality of our lives is a fact that is hard to deny.*

1. It is extremely important that . . . .
2. It is surprising that . . . .
3. That . . . is unfortunate.
4. That . . . indicates that . . . .
5. It is undeniably true that . . . .
6. It seems obvious to me that . . . .
7. That . . . is strange.
8. It is a pity that . . . .
9. I'm not pleased that . . . .
10. It seems necessary that . . . .
11. My biggest problem is that . . . .
12. I'm afraid that . . . . Please try to understand.
13. The reason he was fired from his job is that . . . .
14. That . . . was not made clear to me.
15. The fact that . . . does not mean that . . . .
16. That . . . is amazing.

◇ **PRACTICE 10—SELFSTUDY: Using *the fact that*. (Chart 7-5)**

Directions: Combine each pair of sentences into one sentence by using **the fact that**.

1. I studied for three months for the examination. Regardless of that, I barely passed.
→ *Regardless of **the fact that** I studied for three months for the examination, I barely passed.*

2. Jim lost our tickets to the concert. There's nothing we can do about that.

3. We are going to miss one of the best concerts of the year because of Jim's carelessness. That makes me a little angry.

4. We can't go to the concert. In view of that, let's plan to go to a movie.

5. I couldn't speak a word of Italian and understood very little. Except for that, I had a wonderful time visiting my Italian cousins in Rome.

6. Many people living in Miami speak only Spanish. When I first visited Florida, I was surprised by that.

7. Bobby broke my grandmother's antique flower vase. That isn't important.

8. He lied about it. That is what bothers me.

9. Prof. Brown, who had had almost no teaching experience, was hired to teach the advanced physics courses. At first, some of us objected to that, but she has proven herself to be one of the best.

10. That automobile has the best safety record of any car manufactured this year. I am impressed by that and would definitely recommend that you buy that make.

◇ **PRACTICE 11—SELFSTUDY: Quoted speech. (Chart 7-6)**

Directions: Add the necessary punctuation and capitalization to the following. Do not change the word order or add or delete any words.

1. The athlete said where is my uniform
→ *The athlete said, "Where is my uniform?"*

2. Who won the game asked the spectator

3. Stop the clock shouted the referee we have an injured player

4. I can't remember Margaret said where I put my purse

5. Sandy asked her sister how can I help you get through this difficulty

6. I'll answer your question later he whispered I'm trying to hear what the speaker is saying

7. As the students entered the room, the teacher said please take your seats quickly.

8. Why did I ever take this job Barry wondered aloud

9. After crashing into me and knocking all of my packages to the ground, the man stopped abruptly, turned to me and said softly excuse me

10. I'm going to rest for the next three hours she said I don't want to be disturbed
    That's fine I replied you get some rest I'll make sure no one disturbs you

11. Do we want four more years of corruption and debt the candidate shouted into the microphone no the crowd screamed

12. The woman behind the fast-food counter shouted who's next

   I am three people replied all at the same time

   Which one of you is really next she asked impatiently

   I was here first said a young woman elbowing her way up to the counter I want a hamburger.

   You were not hollered an older man standing next to her I was here before you were give me a

chicken sandwich and a cup of coffee

   Wait a minute I was in line first said a young man give me a cheeseburger and a chocolate shake

   The woman behind the restaurant counter spotted a little boy politely waiting his turn she turned to

him and said hi, Sonny what can I get for you

Directions: Complete the sentences by changing quoted speech to reported speech. Use formal sequence of tenses.

1. Tom said, "I am busy."→ Tom said that he _____ **was** _____ busy.

2. Tom said, "I need some help.→ Tom said that he _____ some help.

3. Tom said, "I am having a good time."→ Tom said that he _____ a good time.

4. Tom said, "I have finished my work."→ Tom said that he _____ his work.

5. Tom said, "I finished it an hour ago."→ Tom said that he _____ it an hour ago.

6. Tom said, "I will arrive at noon."→ Tom said that he _____ at noon.

7. Tom said, "I am going to be there at noon."→ Tom said that he _____ there at noon.

8. Tom said, "I can solve that problem."→ Tom said that he _____ that problem.

9. Tom said, "I may come early."→ Tom said that he _____ early.

10. Tom said, "I might come early."→ Tom said that he _____ early.

11. Tom said, "I must leave at eight."→ Tom said that he _____ at eight.

12. Tom said, "I have to leave at eight."→ Tom said that he _____ at eight.

13. Tom said, "I should go to the library."→ Tom said that he _____ to the library.

14. Tom said, "I ought to go to the library."→ Tom said that he _____ to the library.

15. Tom said, "Stay here."→ Tom told me _____ here.

16. Tom said, "Don't move."→ Tom told me _____.

17. Tom said, "Are you comfortable?"→ Tom asked me if I _____ comfortable.

18. Tom said, "When did you arrive?"→ Tom asked me when I _____.

◇ PRACTICE 13—SELFSTUDY: Reported speech. (Chart 7-7)

Directions: Complete the sentences by changing quoted speech to reported speech. Use formal sequence of tenses as appropriate. (Pay attention to whether the reporting verb is past or present.)

1. *I asked Martha, "Are you planning to enter law school?"*
I asked Martha _____ **if/whether she was planning** _____ to enter law school.

2. Ed just asked me, "What time does the movie begin?"
Ed wants to know _____ **what time the movie begins.** _____

3. *Fred asked, "Can we still get tickets for the concert?"*
Fred asked _____ **if/whether we could still get** _____ tickets for the concert.

4. *Thomas said to us, "How can I help you?"*
Thomas wants to know _____ **how he can help** _____ us.

5. *Eva asked, "Can you help me, John?"*
Eva asked John _____ her.

6. *Charles said, "When will the final decision be made?"*
Charles wanted to know _____

7. *Frank asked Elizabeth, "Where have you been all afternoon?"*

Frank asked Elizabeth _____ all afternoon.

8. *Bill just said, "What is Kim's native language?"*

Bill wants to know _____ .

9. *Yesterday Ron said to Bob, "What's the problem?"*

Ron asked Bob _____ .

10. *I asked myself, "Am I doing the right thing?"*

I wondered _____ the right thing.

11. *All of the farmers are asking, "When is this terrible drought going to end?"*

All of the farmers are wondering _____ to end.

12. *George asked me, "What time do I have to be at the laboratory in the morning?"*

George asked me _____ to be at the laboratory in the morning.

13. *Beth asked, "Who should I give the message to?"*

Beth asked me _____ .

14. *Our tour guide said, "We'll be leaving around 7:00 o'clock in the morning."*

Our tour guide told us _____ around 7:00 o'clock in the morning.

15. *Nancy asked, "Why didn't you call me?"*

Nancy wanted to know _____ her.

◇ **PRACTICE 14—SELFSTUDY: Reported speech. (Chart 7-7)**

Directions: Complete the sentences using the information in the dialogue. Use the formal sequence of tenses.

1. *Fred asked me, "Can we still get tickets to the game?"*
   I said, "I've already bought them."

   When Fred asked me if we _____**could still get**_____ tickets to the game, I told him

   that I _____**had already bought**_____ them.

2. *Mrs. White said, "Janice, you have to clean up your room and empty the dishwasher before you leave for the game."*
   Janice said, "Okay, Mom. I will."

   Mrs. White told Janice that she _____ her room and

   _____ the dishwasher before she _____ for the

   game. Janice promised her mom that she _____ .

3. *I asked Mary, "Why do you still smoke?"*
   Mary replied, "I've tried to quit many times, but I just don't seem to be able to."

   When I asked Mary why she _____ , she replied that she _____

   _____ to quit many times but she just _____ to be able to.

4. *I asked the ticket seller, "Are the concerts going to be rescheduled?"*
   The ticket seller said, "I don't know, Ma'am. I just work here."

   When I asked the ticket seller if the concerts _____ to be rescheduled,

   she told me that she _____ and said that she just _____ there.

5. *The teacher asked, "Bobby, what is the capital of Australia?"*
   Bobby replied, "I'm not sure, but I think it's Sydney."

   Yesterday in class, Bobby's teacher asked him _____. He

   answered that he _____ sure but that he _____ Sydney.

6. *I asked Boris, "Where will the next chess match take place?"*
   Boris replied, "It hasn't been decided yet."

   When I asked Boris _____ place, he replied that it

   _____ yet.

7. *The children inquired of their father, "Will we be able to visit the Air and Space Museum and the Natural History Museum, too?"*
   Their father said, "We will if we leave the hotel before 10 o'clock tomorrow morning."

   The children asked their father whether they _____ able to visit

   the Air and Space Museum and the Natural History Museum, too. He told them they

   _____ if they _____ the hotel before 10 o'clock the next morning.

8. *I said to Alan, "I'm very discouraged. I don't think I'll ever speak English well."*
   Alan said, "Your English is getting better every day. In another year, you'll be speaking English with the greatest of ease."

   I complained that I _____ very discouraged, and that I _____ I

   _____ English well. Alan told me that my English _____

   _____ better every day. He assured me that in another year I _____

   _____ English with the greatest of ease.

9. *I told Jenny, "It's pouring outside. You'd better take an umbrella."*
   Jenny said, "It'll stop soon. I don't need one."

   I told Jenny that it _____ outside and that she _____ an

   umbrella. However, Jenny said she thought the rain _____ soon and that

   she _____ one.

10. *A person in the audience asked the speaker, "Are there presently available the necessary means to increase the world's food supply?"*
    The agronomy professor said, "It might be possible to grow 50 percent of the world's food in underwater cultivation if we can develop inexpensive methods."

    A person in the audience asked the agronomy professor if there _____

    presently available the necessary means to increase the world's food supply. The professor

    stated that it _____ possible to grow 50 percent of the world's food under

    water if we _____ inexpensive methods.

Directions: In the following, read a dialogue and then write a report of the dialogue. In your report, you need to give an accurate idea of the speakers' words, but you don't necessarily have to use the speakers' exact words. Study the first three examples of possible written reports carefully.

Example dialogue:

Jack said, "I can't go to the game."
Tom said, "Oh? Why not?"
Jack replied, "I don't have enough money for a ticket."

Possible written reports of the above dialogue:

→ *Jack told Tom that he couldn't go to the game because he didn't have enough money for a ticket.*

→ *When Tom asked Jack why he couldn't go to the game, Jack said he didn't have enough money for a ticket.*

→ *Jack said he couldn't go to the game. When Tom asked him why not, Jack replied that he didn't have enough money for a ticket.*

Example dialogue:

"Where are you going, Ann?" I asked.
"I'm on my way to the market," she replied. "Do you want to come with me?"
"I'd like to, but I have to stay home. I have a lot of work to do."
"Okay," Ann said. "Is there anything you would like me to pick up for you at the market?"
"How about a few bananas? And some apples if they're fresh?"
"Sure. I'd be happy to."

Possible written report:

→ *When I asked Ann where she was going, she said she was on her way to the market and invited me to come* with her. I said I'd like to, but that I had to stay home because I had a lot of work to do. Ann kindly asked me if there was anything she could pick up for me at the market. I asked her to pick up a few bananas and some apples if they were fresh. She said she'd be happy to.*

Write reports of the following dialogues:

1. "What are you doing?" Alex asked.
   "I'm drawing a picture," I said.

2. Ann said, "Do you want to go to a movie Sunday night?"
   Sue said, "I'd like to, but I have to study."

3. "How old are you, Mrs. Robinson?" the little boy asked.
   Mrs. Robinson said, "It's not polite to ask people their age."

4. "Is there anything you especially want to watch on TV tonight?" my sister asked.
   "Yes." I replied. "There's a show at eight that I've been waiting to see for a long time."
   "What is it?" she asked.
   "It's a documentary on green sea turtles," I said.
   "Why do you want to see that?"
   "I'm doing a research paper on sea turtles. I think I might be able to get some good information from the documentary. Why don't you watch it with me?"
   "No, thanks," she said. "I'd rather do my math homework than watch a show on green sea turtles."

---

*See Chart 4–5 for the use of infinitives to report speech (for example, *invited me **to come**, asked her **to pick up**, told me **to finish**, promised **to do** it*).

◇ **PRACTICE 16—GUIDED STUDY: Reporting speech. (Chapter 7)**

Directions: Break up into small groups and discuss one (or two, or all) of the following topics. At the end of your discussion, make a formal written report of the main points made by each speaker in your group. (Do not attempt to report every word that was spoken.)

In your report, use words such as *think, believe, say, remark,* and *state* to introduce noun clauses. When you use *think* or *believe*, you will probably use present tenses (e.g., *John thinks that money is the most important thing in life.*) When you use *say, remark,* or *state,* you will probably use past tenses (e.g., *Ann said that many other things were more important than money.*).

Do you agree with the given statement? Why or why not?

1. Money is the most important thing in life.
2. A woman can do any job a man can do.
3. When a person decides to get married, his or her love for the other person is the only important consideration.
4. A world government is both desirable and necessary. Countries should simply become the states of one nation, the Earth. In this way, wars could be eliminated and wealth could be equally distributed.

◇ **PRACTICE 17—GUIDED STUDY: Reporting speech. (Chapter 7)**

Directions:

You are a newspaper reporter at a press conference. You and your fellow reporters (your classmates) will interview your teacher or a person whom your teacher invites to class. Your assignment is to write an article for the school newspaper. The purpose of your article is to give a professional and personal sketch of the person whom you interview.

Take notes during the interview. It is important to report information accurately. Listen to the answers carefully. Write down some of the important sentences so that you can use them for quotations in your article. Ask for clarification if you do not understand something the interviewee has said.

When you write the article, try to organize your information into related topics. For example, if you interview your teacher:

    I. General introductory information
    II. Professional life
        A. Present teaching duties
        B. Academic duties and activities outside of teaching
        C. Past teaching experience
        D. Educational background
    III. Personal life
        A. Basic biographical information (e.g., place of birth, family background, places of residence)
        B. Spare-time activities and interests
        C. Travel experiences

The above outline suggests one possible method of organization. You must organize your own article, depending upon the information you learn from the interview and whom you interview.

When you write your report, most of your information will be presented in reported speech; use quoted speech only for the most important or memorable sentences. When you use quoted speech, be sure you are presenting the interviewee's *exact words*. If you are simply paraphrasing what the interviewee said, do not use quotation marks.

◇ **PRACTICE 18—SELFSTUDY: Error analysis. (Chapter 7)**

Directions: The following sentences contain errors. Correct the errors.

1. What is the government official going to say in his speech tonight will affect all of us.
2. I asked Paul help me move the table to the other side of the room.
3. My friend asked me what you are going to do Saturday? I replied it depends on the weather.
4. What my friend and I did it was our secret. We didn't even tell our parents what did we do.
5. The doctor asked that I felt okay. I told him that I don't feel well.
6. Is clear that the ability to use a computer it is an important skill in the modern world.
7. They asked us that we will be sure to turn out the lights when we leave.
8. Is true you almost drowned? my friend asked me.

   Yes, I said. I'm really glad to be alive. It was really frightening.
9. It is a fact that I almost drowned makes me very careful about water safety whenever I go swimming.

◇ **PRACTICE 19—GUIDED STUDY: Error analysis. (Chapter 7)**

Directions: The following sentences contain errors. Correct the errors.

1. I didn't know where am I supposed to get off the bus, so I asked the driver where is the science museum. She tell me the name of the street. She said she will tell me when should I get off the bus.
2. Studying psychology last year made me realize that what kind of career did I want to have.
3. My mother said don't forget your family when you're far away from home.
4. When I asked the taxi driver to drive faster he said I will drive faster if you pay me more. At that time I didn't care how much would it cost, so I told him to go as fast as he can.
5. My mother did not live with us. When other children asked me where was my mother, I told them she is going to come to visit me very soon.
6. I asked him what kind of movies does he like, he said me, I like romantic movies.

◇ **PRACTICE 20—SELFSTUDY: Using the subjunctive. (Chart 7-8)**

Directions: Complete the sentence, using the idea of the words in parentheses.

1. (*You should organize a camping trip.*)
   The girls proposed that their scout leader _____**organize**_____ a camping trip.

2. (*Ms. Hanson thinks that the director should divide our class into two sections.*)
   Ms. Hanson recommended that our class _____**be divided**_____ into two sections.

3. (*You must call home every week.*)
   Dan's parents insisted that he _____ home every week.

4. (*Someone must tell her the truth about her illness.*)

It is essential that she _____ the truth about her illness.

5. (*Open your suitcases for inspection.*)

The customs official demanded that all passengers _____ their suitcases.

6. (*Ann, you should take some art courses.*)

The counselor recommended that Ann _____ some art courses.

7. (*All parts of the motor must work correctly.*)

It is vital that all parts of the motor _____ in proper working order.

8. (*Please mail all packages at the central office.*)

The director requests that all packages _____ at the central office.

9. (*Soldiers must obey their officers.*)

It is imperative that soldiers _____ their officers.

10. (*We must remember to give the babysitter certain phone numbers to call in case of emergency.*)

It is important that the babysitter _____ phone numbers to call in case of emergency.

◇ **PRACTICE 21—SELFSTUDY: Using -*ever* words. (Chart 7-9)**

Directions: Complete the following sentences by using -*ever* words.

1. As vice-president of international sales, Robert has complete control over his travel schedule. He can travel _____*whenever*_____ he wants.

2. Robert is free to decide which countries he will visit during his overseas trips. He can travel _____*wherever*_____ he wants.

3. The English professor told us that we could write our papers on _____ subject we wanted as long as it related to the topics we discussed in class this semester.

4. There are only two appointment time slots remaining. You may select _____ one you prefer.

5. To Ellen, the end justifies the means. She will do _____ she has to do in order to accomplish her objective.

6. Linda is very amiable and gregarious. She makes friends with _____ she meets.

7. It doesn't matter which class you take to fulfill this requirement. Just take _____ one fits best into your schedule.

8. _____ is the last to leave the room should turn off the lights and lock the door.

9. I know that Norman will succeed. He'll do _____ is required to succeed.

10. My wife and I are going to ride our bicycles across the country. We will ride for six to seven hours every day, then stop _____ we happen to be at the end of the day.

◇ **PRACTICE TEST A—SELFSTUDY: Noun clauses. (Chapter 7)**

Directions: In each of the following, select the ONE correct answer.

Example:
He asked me where __**B**__.
   A. *did I live*   B. *I lived*   C. *do you live*   D. *that I lived*

1. I talked to Bob two weeks ago. I thought he wanted to know about my cat, but I misunderstood him. He asked me where _____, not my cat.
   A. is my hat   B. my hat was   C. my hat is   D. was my hat

2. "The people in the apartment upstairs must have a lot of children."
"I don't know how many _____, but it sounds like they have a dozen."
   A. children do they have   B. do they have children
   C. children they have   D. they have children

3. Do you know _____? I myself have no idea.
   A. how many years the earth is   B. how old the earth is
   C. how long is the earth   D. how much time has been the earth

4. "There's too much noise in this room. I can't understand what _____."
"Neither can I."
   A. is the professor saying   B. is saying the professor
   C. that the professor is saying   D. the professor is saying

5. When I was little, my father gave me some advice. He said _____ talk to strangers.
   A. I shouldn't   B. that shouldn't   C. don't   D. that I don't

6. "I didn't expect Ann's husband to be here at the opera with her."
"I'm surprised, too. Ann must have insisted that _____ with her."
   A. he come   B. he comes   C. he came   D. he had come

7. "Ms. Wright, can you give me a little extra help typing some letters today?"
"Sorry, I can't. The boss has an urgent report for me to write. She demanded that it _____ on her desk by 5 P.M. today."
   A. was   B. will be   C. is   D. be

8. "Did you tell Carol where _____ us this evening?"
"Yes, I did. I can't understand why she is late."
   A. should she meet   B. she to meet   C. she meets   D. to meet

9. A fortune-teller predicted _____ inherit a lot of money before the end of the year.
   A. that I would   B. that I   C. what I will   D. what I

10. "Bill Frazer seems like a good person for the job, but we don't know why he left his last job."
"I know why. He told me _____ a serious policy disagreement with his boss last January."
   A. if he'd had   B. he'd had   C. what he'd had   D. that what he had

11. "Is it true that you fell asleep in class yesterday and began to snore?"
"Unfortunately, yes. _____ is unbelievable! I'm very embarrassed."
   A. That I could do such a thing it   B. That I could do such a thing
   C. I could do such a thing it   D. I could do such a thing

12. "Officer, can you tell me how to get to Springfield?"
"Sure. What part of Springfield _____ to go to?"
   A. do you want   B. you want   C. that you want   D. where you want

13. "Is it true _____ the law says there is no smoking in restaurants in this city?"
"Yes. That law was passed last year."
   A. that what   B. what   C. if   D. that

14. _____ prompt is important to our boss.
    A. A person is   B. Is a person   C. If a person is   D. Whether or not a person is

15. A scientific observer of wildlife must note every detail of how _____ in their environment: their eating and sleeping habits, their social relationships, and their methods of self-protection.
    A. do animals live   B. live animals   C. do live animals   D. animals live

16. The mystery movie was clever and suspenseful. The audience couldn't guess _____ committed the murder until the surprise ending.
    A. who he   B. who had   C. that who   D. that

17. How do you like your new school? Tell me _____.
    A. who in your class is   B. who your class is in
    C. who is in your class   D. your class who is in it

18. "What do you recommend _____ about this tax problem?"
"I strongly suggest that we consult an expert as soon as possible."
    A. do we do   B. we will do   C. we do   D. should we do

19. The college does not grant degrees simply to _____ pays the cost of tuition; the student must satisfy the academic requirements.
    A. whoever   B. who   C. whomever   D. whoever that

20. "What are you going to buy in this store?"
"Nothing. _____ want is much too expensive."
    A. That I   B. What I   C. That what I   D. What do I

◇ **PRACTICE TEST B—GUIDED STUDY: Noun clauses. (Chapter 7)**

Directions: In each of the following, select the ONE correct answer.

Example:
*He asked me where __**B**__.*
    A. did I live   *B. I lived*   *C. do you live*   *D. that I lived*

1. "Does anybody know _____ on the ground?"
"Your guess is as good as mine."
    A. how long this plane will be   B. how long will be this plane
    C. how long will this plane be   D. that how long this plane will be

2. "This restaurant is very expensive!"
"It is, but order _____ want. Your birthday is a very special occasion."
    A. what is it you   B. what do you   C. whatever you   D. whatever you do

3. Why did Beth ask you _____ a bicycle?
    A. that if you had   B. do you have   C. that you had   D. if you had

4. "What did your grammar teacher want to talk to you about?"
"I did badly on the last test. She _____ study for it."
    A. said why didn't I   B. asked why didn't I
    C. said why I didn't   D. asked why I didn't

5. "Why are you staring out the window? What _____ about?"
"Nothing."
    A. you are thinking   B. you think
    C. are you thinking   D. do you are thinking

6. "I can't decide what color I want for my bedroom. What do you think?"
"You should choose _____ color you want. You're the one who will have to live with it."
  A. whichever that B. whatever   C. however   D. that what

7. "Did you remember to tell Marge _____ she should bring to the meeting tomorrow?"
"Oh, my gosh! I completely forgot! I'm sorry."
  A. that   B. what   C. if   D. that what

8. "My aunt has been feeling bad since Uncle George died. Is it because she's depressed?"
"I think so. _____ can cause debilitating physical symptoms is a medical fact."
  A. Depression   B. That depression it
  C. That depression   D. It is that depression

9. There was an earthquake on the coast yesterday. Fortunately, there was no loss of life. However, because of the danger of collapsing sea walls, it was essential that the area _____ evacuated quickly.
  A. to be   B. will be   C. be   D. is

10. _____ saying was so important that I asked everyone to stop talking and listen.
  A. What the woman was   B. The woman was
  C. That the woman was   D. What was the woman

11. "This cake is terrible. What happened?"
"It's my grandmother's recipe, but she forgot to tell me how long _____ it."
  A. did I bake   B. should I bake   C. do I bake   D. to bake

12. "Let's go to Riverton this weekend."
"Sounds like fun. _____ from here?"
  A. How far is   B. How far it is   C. It how far is   D. How far is it

13. "Somebody forgot this hat. I wonder _____."
  A. whose is this hat B. whose hat this is C. whose hat is D. is this whose hat

14. Edward's interview was very intense. The interviewer wanted to know many facts about his personal life, and even asked him _____ had ever used any illegal drugs of any kind.
  A. that if he   B. that he   C. if or not he   D. whether or not he

15. It is hoped that all present-day communicable diseases will be conquered. However, _____ about certain diseases is still not sufficient to prevent them from spreading easily among the population.
  A. what we know   B. what do we know
  C. what we know that   D. that we know what

16. "Why didn't Henry attend the meeting this morning?"
"He's been very sick. His doctor insisted that he _____ in bed this week."
  A. will stay   B. stayed   C. stays   D. stay

17. Nobody yet knew what _____ to cause the dam to burst, but the residents of the area organized quickly to protect life and property against the rising floods.
  A. happens   B. had happened C. happen   D. did it happen

18. Did the teacher explain how _____ this problem?
  A. do we solve   B. can we solve   C. to solve   D. solve

19. _____ the National Weather Bureau predicted severe storms did not deter the fishing boats from going out into the open seas.
  A. The fact that   B. That fact is that   C. Is fact that   D. The fact is that

20. Tom walked into the huge hall to register for classes. At first, he simply looked around and wondered what _____ supposed to do.
  A. was he   B. am I   C. he was   D. I am

CHAPTER 8
Showing Relationships Between Ideas—Part I

◇ **PRACTICE 1—SELFSTUDY: Parallel structure. (Chart 8-1)**

Directions: Write the words that are parallel in each of the sentences.

1. These apples are fresh and sweet.

    1. _____***fresh***_____ and _____***sweet***_____
         (adjective)   +   (adjective)

2. These apples and pears are fresh.

    2. _____ and _____
         (noun)   +   (noun)

3. I washed and dried the apples.

    3. _____ and _____
         (verb)   +   (verb)

4. I am washing and drying the apples.

    4. _____ and _____
         (verb)   +   (verb)

5. We ate the fruit happily and quickly.

    5. _____ and _____
         (adverb)   +   (adverb)

6. I enjoy biting into a fresh apple and tasting the juicy sweetness.

    6. _____ and _____
         (gerund)   +   (gerund)

7. I like to bite into a fresh apple and taste the juicy sweetness.

    7. _____ and _____
         (infinitive)   +   (infinitive)

8. Those imported apples are delicious but expensive.

    8. _____ but _____
         (adjective)   +   (adjective)

9. Apples, pears, and bananas are kinds of fruit.

    9. _____, _____, and _____
         (noun) + (noun) + (noun)

10. Those apples are red, ripe, and juicy.

    10. _____, _____, and _____
        (adjective) + (adjective) + (adjective)

◇ **PRACTICE 2—SELFSTUDY: Parallel structure. (Charts 8-1 and 8-2)**

Directions: Write "C" if the parallel structure is CORRECT. Write "I" if the parallel structure is INCORRECT, and make any necessary corrections. Underline the parallel elements of the sentences.

                                                                  honesty

1. __**I**__ I admire him for his <u>intelligence</u>, cheerful <u>disposition</u>, and ~~he is honest~~.

2. __**C**__ Abraham Lincoln was a <u>lawyer</u> and a <u>politician</u>.

3. _____ When Anna moved, she had to rent an apartment, make new friends, and find a job.

4. _____ Barb studies each problem carefully and works out a solution.

5. _____ Aluminum is plentiful and relatively inexpensive.

6. _____ Many visitors to Los Angeles enjoy visiting Disneyland and to tour movie studios.

7. _____ Children are usually interested in but a little frightened by snakes.

8. _____ Either fainting can result from a lack of oxygen or a loss of blood.

9. _____ So far this term, the students in the writing class have learned how to write thesis statements, organize their material, and summarizing their conclusions.

10. _____ The boat sailed across the lake smoothly and quiet.

11. _____ When I looked more closely, I saw that it was not coffee but chocolate on my necktie.

12. _____ Not only universities support medical research but also many government agencies.

13. _____ Physics explains why water freezes and how the sun produces heat.

14. _____ All plants need light, a suitable climate, and an ample supply of water and minerals from the soil.

15. _____ With their keen sight, fine hearing, and refined sense of smell, wolves hunt day or night in quest of elk, deer, moose, or caribou.

◇ PRACTICE 3—SELFSTUDY: Paired conjunctions, subject-verb agreement. (Chart 8-2)

Directions: Supply the correct present tense form of the verb in parentheses.

1. (know)   Neither the students nor the teacher _____ *knows* _____ the answer.

2. (know)   Neither the teacher nor the students _____ *know* _____ the answer.

3. (know)   Not only the students but also the teacher _____ the answer.

4. (know)   Not only the teacher but also the students _____ the answer.

5. (know)   Both the teacher and the student _____ the answer.

6. (want)   Neither Alan nor Carol _____ to go skiing this weekend.

7. (like)   Both John and Ted _____ to go cross-country skiing.

8. (have)   Either Jack or Alice _____ the information you need.

9. (agree)   Neither my parents nor my brother _____ with my decision.

10. (be)   Both intelligence and skill _____ essential to good teaching.

11. (realize)   Neither my classmates nor my teacher _____ that I have no idea what's going on in class.

12. (think)   Not only Laura's husband but also her children _____ she should return to school and finish her graduate degree.

◇ PRACTICE 4—SELFSTUDY: Paired conjunctions. (Chart 8-2)

Directions: Combine the following into sentences which contain parallel structure. Use the paired conjunctions in parentheses. Pay special attention to the exact place you put the paired conjunctions in the combined sentence.

1. Many people don't drink coffee. Many people don't drink alcohol. (neither . . . nor)
   → *Many people drink neither coffee nor alcohol.*

2. Barbara is fluent in Chinese. She is also fluent in Japanese. (not only . . . but also)

3. I'm sorry to say that Paul has no patience. He has no sensitivity to others. (neither . . . nor)

4. She can sing. She can dance. (*both . . . and*)

5. If you want to change your class schedule, you should talk to your teacher, or you should talk to your academic counselor. (*either . . . or*)

6. Diana is intelligent. She is very creative. (*both . . . and*)

7. You may begin working tomorrow or you may begin next week. (*either . . . or*)

8. Michael didn't tell his mother about the trouble he had gotten into. He didn't tell his father about the trouble he had gotten into. (*neither . . . nor*)

9. Success in karate requires balance and skill. Success in karate requires concentration and mental alertness. (*not only . . . but also*)

◇ **PRACTICE 5—GUIDED STUDY: Parallel structure. (Charts 8-1 and 8-2)**

Directions: With your own words, complete the sentences using parallel structures.

1. Dennis has proven himself to be a sincere, hardworking, and _____*efficient*_____ supervisor.

2. The professor walked through the door and _____.

3. I was listening to music and _____ when I heard a knock at the door.

4. I'm planning to stay here during the summer but _____ in the winter.

5. When I was a student, I would usually _____ and then _____ after dinner.

6. _____ and attending concerts in the park are two of the things my wife and I like to do on summer weekends.

7. When you visit other countries, it is important to be able to speak at least a few words of the language, to understand the local customs, and _____.

8. I get up at seven every morning, eat a light breakfast, and _____.

9. Our whole family enjoys camping. We especially enjoy fishing in mountain streams and _____.

10. My parents want me to either call or _____ every week, but I'm so busy and _____ by the end of each day that all I want to do is go to bed and _____.

11. You can pay the bill either _____ or _____.

12. I'm going to subscribe to either _____ or _____.

◇ **PRACTICE 6—GUIDED STUDY: Parallel structure. (Charts 8-1 and 8-2)**

Directions: Choose the correct completion in parentheses.

1. *Hamlet* is one of Shakespeare's finest and most (*famous*, *famously*) plays.

2. On my vacation I lost a suitcase, broke my glasses, and (*missing*, *missed*) my plane.

3. Walking briskly for 30 minutes or (*run*, *running*) for 15 minutes will burn an approximately equal number of calories.

4. Slowly and (*cautious*, *cautiously*), the firefighter ascended the charred staircase.

5. The comedian made people laugh by telling jokes and (*making*, *make*) funny faces.

6. Tina is always understanding, patient, and (*speaks sensitively*, *sensitive*) when helping her friends with their problems.

7. Not only the post office but also all banks (*closes*, *close*) on most national holidays.

8. When tourists visit a new city, they often have trouble deciding where to go and how (*they can get*, *to get*) there.

9. Both the Indian cobra snake and the king cobra (*uses*, *use*) poison from their fangs in two ways: by injecting it directly into their prey or (*spit*, *by spitting*) it into the eyes of the victim.

10. What do people in your country think of bats? Are they mean and (*scary*, *scare*) creatures, or are they symbols of happiness and (*lucky*, *good luck*)? In western countries, many people have an unreasoned fear of bats. According to scientist Dr. Sharon Horowitz, bats are beneficial and (*harmless*, *harm*) mammals. "When I was a child, I believed that a bat would attack me and (*tangle*, *tangled*) itself in my hair. Now I know better," said Dr. Horowitz.

   Contrary to popular western myths, bats do not attack humans and (*be*, *are*) not blind. Though a few bats may be infected, they are not major carriers of rabies or (*give people other dread diseases*, *other dread diseases*). Bats help natural plant life by pollinating plants, (*spread seeds, and eat insects; spreading seeds, and eating insects*). If you get rid of bats that eat overripe fruit, then fruit flies flourish and (*destroying*, *can destroy*) the fruit industry. According to Dr. Horowitz, they make loving, trainable, and (*gentle*, *gently*) pets. Not many people, however, are known to have bats as pets, and bats themselves prefer to avoid people.

◇ **PRACTICE 7—SELFSTUDY:** Combining independent clauses: periods and commas. (Charts 8-1 and 8-3)

Directions: Punctuate the following sentences by adding periods (.) or commas (,) as necessary. Do not add any words. Capitalize letters where necessary. Some sentences may require no changes.

1. I like French cooking my wife prefers Italian cooking.
   → *I like French cooking. My wife prefers Italian cooking.*

2. I like French cooking but my wife prefers Italian cooking.
   → *I like French cooking, but my wife prefers Italian cooking. (optional comma)*

3. I've read that book it's very good.

4. I've read that book but I didn't like it.

5. I opened the door and asked my friend to come in.

6. I opened the door my sister answered the phone.

7. I opened the door and my sister answered the phone.

8. Minerals are common materials they are found in rocks and soil.

9. The most common solid materials on earth are minerals they are found in rocks soil and water.

10. You can travel to England by plane or you can go by ship if you prefer.

11. You can travel to England by plane or by ship.

12. Jason was going to study all night so he declined our invitation to dinner.

13. Jason declined our invitation to dinner he needed to stay home and study.

14. The wind was howling outside yet it was warm and comfortable indoors.

15. I hurried to answer the phone for I didn't want the children to wake up.

16. Last weekend we went camping it rained the entire time.

17. The highway was under construction so we had to take a different route to work.

18. No one thought we would win the championship yet our team won by a large margin.

19. We arrived at the theatre late but the play had not yet begun we were quite surprised.

20. A central heating system provides heat for an entire building from one central place most central heating systems service only one building but some systems heat a group of buildings, such as those at a military base a campus or an apartment complex.

◇ **PRACTICE 8—GUIDED STUDY:** Using parallel structure. (Charts 8-1 → 8-3)

Directions: Write two descriptive paragraphs on one of the topics below. The first paragraph should be a draft, and the second should be a "tightened up" revision of the same description. Look for places where two or three sentences can be combined into one by effective use of parallel structure. Pay special attention to punctuation and be sure all of your commas and periods are used correctly.

Topics: 1. Give a physical description of your place of residence (apartment, dorm room, etc.).
2. Describe the characteristics and activities of a successful student.
3. Give your reader directions for making a particular food dish.

Example:

First draft: *To make spaghetti sauce, you will need several ingredients. First, you will need some ground beef. Probably about one pound of ground beef will be sufficient. You should also have an onion. If the onions are small, you should use two. Also, find a green pepper and put it in the sauce. Of course, you will also need some tomato sauce or tomatoes.*

Revision: *To make spaghetti sauce you will need one pound of ground beef, one large or two small onions, a green pepper, and some tomato sauce or tomatoes.*

◇ PRACTICE 9—SELFSTUDY: Adverb clauses. (Chart 8-4)

Directions: Change the position of the adverb clause in the sentence. Underline the adverb clause in the given sentence, and underline the adverb clause in the new sentence. Punctuate carefully.

1. As soon as a hurricane strikes land, its force begins to diminish.
   → *A hurricane's force begins to diminish as soon as it strikes land.*

2. I didn't feel any older when I reached my 21st birthday.
   → *When I reached my 21st birthday, I didn't feel any older.*

3. I had a cup of tea before I left for work.

4. After I get home from work, I like to read the evening newspaper.

5. Since my watch broke, I have been late to work three times.

6. My cat hides under the house whenever it rains.

7. I'm going to get a job once I finish school.

8. While I was waiting for my bus, I heard a gunshot.

9. The village will have no electric power until a new generator is installed.

10. The last time I was in Taipei, I saw Mr. Wu.

11. Because I already had my boarding pass, I didn't have to stand in line at the airline counter.

12. Productivity in a factory increases if the workplace is made pleasant.

◇ PRACTICE 10—SELFSTUDY: Periods and commas. (Charts 8-1 → 8-5)

Directions: Add periods and commas as necessary. Do not change, add, or omit any words. Capitalize as necessary.

1. The lake was calm Tom went fishing.
   → *The lake was calm. Tom went fishing.*

2. Because the lake was calm Tom went fishing.
   → *Because the lake was calm, Tom went fishing.*

3. Tom went fishing because the lake was calm he caught two fish.

4. Tom went fishing because the lake was calm and caught two fish.

5. When Tom went fishing the lake was calm he caught two fish.

6. The lake was calm so Tom went fishing he caught two fish.

7. Because the lake was calm and quiet Tom went fishing.

8. The lake was calm quiet and clear when Tom went fishing.

◇ PRACTICE 11—GUIDED STUDY: Periods and commas. (Charts 8-1 → 8-5; 6-8)

Directions: Add periods and commas as necessary. Do not change, add, or omit any words. Capitalize as necessary.

1. Mr. Hood is admired because he dedicated his life to helping the poor he is well known for his work on behalf of homeless people.

2. Greg Adams has been blind since he was two years old today he is a key scientist in a computer company he is able to design complex electronic equipment because he can depend

on a computer that reads writes and speaks out loud his blindness neither helps nor hinders him it is largely irrelevant to how well he does his job.

3. Microscopes automobile dashboards and cameras are awkward for lefthanded people to use they are designed for righthanded people when ''lefties'' use these items they have to use their right hand to do the things that they would normally do with their left hand.

4. When you speak to someone who is hard of hearing you do not have to shout it is important to face the person directly and to speak clearly my father who is hard of hearing and wears a hearing aid can understand me if I speak distinctly as long as I enunciate clearly I do not need to shout when I speak to him.

◇ PRACTICE 12—SELFSTUDY: Verb tenses in adverb clauses of time. (Chart 8-5; Chapter 1)

Directions: Choose the letter of the correct answer.

1. After Jessica __C__ her degree, she intends to work in her father's company.
   A. will finish   B. will have finished   C. finishes   D. is finishing

2. By the time I go to bed tonight, I _____ my work for the day.
   A. will finish   B. have finished   C. will have finished   D. finish

3. When my parents _____ for a visit tomorrow, they will see our new baby for the first time.
   A. will arrive   B. arrived   C. will have arrived   D. arrive

4. Fatemah looked down to discover a snake at her feet. When she saw it, she _____.
   A. was screaming   B. had screamed   C. screamed   D. screams

5. By the time Alfonso finally graduated from high school, he _____ seven different schools because his parents moved frequently.
   A. attended   B. was attending   C. had attended   D. had been attending

6. Until you learn to relax more, you _____ your ability to speak English.
   A. haven't improved   B. aren't improving   C. don't improve   D. won't improve

7. I borrowed four books on gardening the last time I _____ to the library.
   A. go   B. went   C. had gone   D. have gone

8. Before I started the car, all of the passengers _____ their seat belts.
   A. will buckle   B. had buckled   C. buckle   D. have buckled

9. It seems that whenever I travel abroad I _____ to take something I need.
   A. forgot   B. am forgetting   C. forget   D. had forgotten

10. When I see the doctor this afternoon, I _____ him to look at my throat.
    A. will ask   B. asked   C. will have asked   D. ask

11. After ancient Greek athletes won a race in the Olympics, they _____ a simple crown of olive leaves.
    A. received   B. had received   C. were receiving   D. have received

12. After the race _____, the celebration began.
    A. had been won   B. is won   C. will be won   D. has been won

13. I'll return Bob's pen to him the next time I _____ him.
    A. see   B. will see   C. will have seen   D. have seen

14. I _____ all of the questions correctly since I began this grammar exercise on verb tenses.
   A. am answering   B. answer   C. have answered   D. answered

15. A small stone struck the windshield while we _____ down the gravel road.
   A. drive   B. were driving   C. had driven   D. had been driving

◇ **PRACTICE 13—GUIDED STUDY: Verb tenses in adverb clauses of time. (Chart 8-5; Chapter 1)**

Directions: Choose the letter of the correct answer.

1. As soon as Martina saw the fire, she _____ the fire department.
   A. was telephoning   B. telephoned   C. had telephoned   D. telephones

2. Before Jennifer won the lottery, she _____ any kind of contest.
   A. hasn't entered   B. didn't enter   C. wasn't entering   D. hadn't entered

3. Every time Prakash sees a movie made in India, he _____ homesick.
   A. will have felt   B. felt   C. feels   D. is feeling

4. Since I left Venezuela six years ago, I _____ to visit friends and family several times.
   A. return   B. will have returned   C. am returning   D. have returned

5. While he was washing his new car, Mr. De Rosa _____ a small dent in the rear fender.
   A. has discovered   B. was discovering   C. is discovering   D. discovered

6. Yesterday while I was jogging in the park, Matthew _____ on the company's annual report.
   A. was working   B. had been working   C. has worked   D. works

7. Tony _____ to have children until his little daughter was born. After she won his heart, he
   decided he wanted a big family.
   A. didn't want   B. hadn't wanted   C. wasn't wanting   D. hasn't wanted

8. After the horse threw her to the ground for the third time, Jennifer picked herself up and said,
   "I _____ on another horse as long as I live."
   A. never ride   B. have never ridden   C. will never ride   D. do not ride

9. The next time Paul _____ to New York, he will visit the Metropolitan Museum's famous
   collection of international musical instruments.
   A. will fly   B. flies   C. has flown   D. will have flown

10. Ever since Maurice arrived, he _____ quietly in the corner. Is something wrong?
   A. sat   B. has been sitting   C. sits   D. is sitting

11. After Nancy _____ for twenty minutes, she began to feel tired.
   A. jogging   B. had been jogging   C. has been jogging   D. has jogged

12. Peter, _____ since you got home from football practice?
   A. have you eaten   B. will you eat   C. are you eating   D. do you eat

13. By the time the young birds _____ the nest for good, they will have learned how to fly.
   A. will leave   B. will have left   C. are leaving   D. leave

14. The last time I _____ in Athens, the weather was hot and humid.
   A. had been   B. was   C. am   D. will be

15. The farmer acted too late. He locked the barn door after his horse _____.
   A. had been stolen   B. will be stolen   C. is stolen   D. has been stolen

◇ **PRACTICE 14—SELFSTUDY:** Using adverb clauses to show time relationships. (Chart 8-5)

Directions: Combine each pair of sentences into one new sentence using the word(s) in parentheses. Omit unnecessary words, make any necessary changes, and punctuate carefully. Pay special attention to verb tenses. <u>Underline</u> the adverb clause in the new sentence.

1. The other passengers will get on the bus soon. Then we'll leave. (*as soon as*)
   → <u>**As soon as** the other passengers get on the bus</u>, we'll leave.

2. I turned off the lights. After that, I left the room. (*before*)
   → I turned off the lights <u>**before** I left the room</u>.

3. Susan sometimes feels nervous. Then she chews her nails. (*whenever*)

4. I saw the great pyramids of Egypt in the moonlight. I was speechless then. (*the first time*)

5. The frying pan caught on fire. I was making dinner at that time. (*while*)

6. I'll finish working on the car soon. Then we'll all take a walk in the park. (*as soon as*)

7. Ceylon had been independent for 24 years. Then its name was changed to Sri Lanka. (*after*)

8. Shakespeare died in 1616. He had written more than 37 plays before then. (*by the time*)

9. Douglas fell off his bicycle last week. He has had to use crutches to walk. (*since*)

10. Ms. Johnson will return your call soon. She'll have some free time soon. (*as soon as*)

11. John will learn how to use a computer. Then he'll be able to work more efficiently. (*once*)

12. I won't return my book to the library. I'll finish my research project first. (*until*)

13. Sue dropped a carton of eggs. She was leaving the store. (*as*)

14. Sam will go to the movies again. He'll remember to take his glasses then. (*the next time*)

15. The flooding river raced down the valley. It destroyed everything in its path. (*when*)

16. Mohammad had never heard about Halloween.* Then he came to the United States. (*before*)

---

*Halloween (which occurs every year on October 31) is a U.S. holiday primarily for children, who dress up in costumes and go from house to house for a "treat" such as candy or fruit.

◇ **PRACTICE 15—GUIDED STUDY:** Using adverb clauses to show time relationships. (Chart 8-5)

Directions: Write a sentence from the given words. Do not change the order of the words. Use any appropriate verb forms and punctuate carefully.

Examples:
> as soon as + I + finish + I → ***As soon as I finish*** *my report,* ***I'll*** *call you and we'll go to dinner.*
> I + after + I + climb → *I was exhausted* ***after I climbed*** *the stairs to the eighth floor.*

1. whenever + I + go + I
2. by the time + I + get + I
3. I + since + I + leave
4. just as + I + open + I
5. I + as soon as + I + eat

6. I + when + I + be
7. the first time + I + see + I
8. I + until + I + be
9. while + I + look + I
10. I + before + I + drive

◇ **PRACTICE 16—SELFSTUDY:** Cause and effect. (Charts 8-1, 8-4, 8-6 → 8-11)

Directions: Choose **ALL** of the correct completions for each sentence. There may be more than one correct answer.

Example:
> ___**B, D**___ *the post office was closed, I couldn't mail my packages.*
> A. Therefore   B. Because   C. For   D. Since

1. _____ we got lost driving into the city, we were late for the meeting.
   A. Since   B. Because   C. Consequently   D. For

2. I couldn't repair my bicycle, _____ I didn't have the right tools.
   A. so   B. for   C. because of   D. therefore

3. Two of the factories in our small town have closed. _____, unemployment is high.
   A. Consequently   B. Because   C. So that   D. Therefore

4. _____ I had nothing for lunch but an apple, I ate dinner early.
   A. For   B. Since   C. Due to   D. Therefore

5. The fire raged out of control. It got _____ bad that more firefighters had to be called in.
   A. such   B. therefore   C. so   D. as

6. _____ the flood has receded, people can move back into their homes.
   A. Now that   B. Since   C. Because   D. Inasmuch as

7. Mr. Watson retired from his job early _____ his ill health.
   A. because   B. due to   C. because of   D. for

8. Bill's favorite show was on. He reached to turn on the TV _____ he could watch it.
   A. because of   B. therefore   C. so that   D. for

9. She bought the book _____ she had heard it was good.
   A. because   B. so   C. because of   D. due to the fact that

10. The Eskimo* way of life changed dramatically during the 1800s _____ the introduction of firearms and the influx of large numbers of European whalers and fur traders.
    A. because   B. due to   C. so   D. for

---
*Eskimos are people who live in the Arctic regions of northern Alaska, northern Canada, and Greenland.

11. During extremely hot weather, elephants require both mud and water to keep their skin cool _____ they have no sweat glands.

    A. and   B. so   C. because of   D. due to the fact that

12. Tommy doesn't have Ms. Simmons as his fifth grade teacher anymore. _____ the classroom was overcrowded, Tommy and several other children were assigned to a different class.

    A. Because   B. Therefore   C. For   D. Due to

◇ **PRACTICE 17—SELFSTUDY: Using adverb clauses to show cause and effect relationships. (Chart 8-6)**

Directions: Combine the sentences, using the word or phrase in parentheses. Add commas where necessary.

1. We can go swimming every day. The weather is warm. (*now that*)
   → *We can go swimming every day* ***now that the weather is warm.***

2. All of the students had done poorly on the test. The teacher decided to give it again. (*since*)
   → ***Since all of the students had done poorly on the test,*** *the teacher decided to give it again.*

3. Cold air hovers near the earth. It is heavier than hot air. (*because*)

4. Our TV set was broken. We listened to the news on the radio. (*because*)

5. Larry is finally caught up on his work. He can start his vacation tomorrow. (*now that*)

6. You have paid for the theater tickets. Please let me pay for our dinner. (*inasmuch as*)

7. 92,000 people already have reservations with Pan Am for a trip to the moon. I doubt that I'll get the chance to go on one of the first tourist flights. (*since*)

8. Our flight is going to be delayed. Let's relax and enjoy a quiet dinner. (*as long as*)

9. My registration is going to be canceled. I haven't paid my fees. (*because*)

10. Erica has qualified for the Olympics in speedskating. She must train even more vigorously. (*now that*)

◇ PRACTICE 18—SELFSTUDY: Using *because* and *because of.* (Charts 8-6 and 8-7)

Directions: Complete the sentences with either *because* or *because of.*

1. We postponed our trip ____*because of*____ the bad driving conditions.

2. Sue's eyes were red ____*because*____ she had been swimming in a chlorinated pool.

3. We can't visit the museum tomorrow _____ it isn't open.

4. Jim had to give up jogging _____ his sprained ankle.

5. _____ heavy fog at the airport, we had to stay in Boston an extra day.

6. _____ the elevator was broken, we had to walk up six flights of stairs.

7. Please walk carefully _____ the walkway is slippery when wet.

8. Thousands of Irish people emigrated to the United States _____ the potato famine in Ireland in the middle of the nineteenth century.

9. The young couple decided not to buy the house _____ its dilapidated condition.

10. You can't enter this secured area _____ you don't have an official permit.

11. My lecture notes were incomplete _____ the instructor talked too fast.

12. _____ the re-opening of the only factory in town, most of the residents of Waterton are working again.

◇ PRACTICE 19—GUIDED STUDY: Using *because* and *therefore.* (Charts 8-6 and 8-8)

Directions: Combine the given sentences in two ways: (a) use *because*; (b) use *therefore*. Punctuate and capitalize as appropriate.

1. John didn't go to work yesterday. He didn't feel well.

   (a) *because* → *John didn't go to work yesterday* **because** *he didn't feel well.*
       OR: **Because** *John didn't feel well, he didn't go to work yesterday.*

   (b) *therefore* → *John didn't feel well.* **Therefore,** *he didn't go to work yesterday.*
       OR: *John didn't feel well. He,* **therefore,** *didn't go to work yesterday.*
       OR: *John didn't feel well. He didn't go to work yesterday,* **therefore.**

2. Angela ate a sandwich. She was hungry.

3. We need to eat nutritious food. Good health is important.

4. Edward missed the final exam. He failed the course.

5. Jessica secured a good job in international business. She is bilingual.

◇ **PRACTICE 20—SELFSTUDY: Using *because* and *therefore*. (Charts 8-6 and 8-8)**

Directions: Add appropriate punctuation and capitalization as necessary.

1. Bill couldn't pick us up for the concert because his car wouldn't start. (*no changes*)

2. Bill's car wouldn't start therefore he couldn't pick us up for the concert.
   → *Bill's car wouldn't start. Therefore, he couldn't pick us up for the concert.*

3. Because young Joseph was an inquisitive student he was always liked by his teachers.

4. Emily has never wanted to return to the Yukon to live because the winters are too severe.

5. We lose 60 percent of our body heat through our head therefore it is important to wear a hat on cold days.

6. The television broadcast was interrupted in the middle of the eighth inning therefore most of the audience missed the conclusion of the baseball game.

7. When I was in my teens and twenties it was easy for me to get into an argument with my father because both of us have always been stubborn and opinionated.

8. Robert did not pay close attention to what the travel agent said when he went to see her at her office last week therefore he had to ask many of the same questions again the next time he talked to her.

◇ **PRACTICE 21—SELFSTUDY: Showing cause and effect. (Charts 8-6 → 8-9)**

PART I: Complete the sentences with *because of*, *because*, or *therefore*. Add any necessary punctuation and capitalization.

1. _____*Because*_____ it rained, we stayed home.

2. It rained _____. *Therefore*,_____ we stayed home.

3. We stayed home _____*because of*_____the rain.

4. The hurricane was moving directly toward a small coastal town _____ all residents were advised to move inland until it passed.

5. The residents moved inland _____ the hurricane.

6. _____ the hurricane was moving directly toward the town all residents were advised to move inland.

7. Piranhas, which are found in the Amazon River, are ferocious and bloodthirsty fish. When they attack in great numbers, they can devour an entire cow in several minutes _____ their extremely sharp teeth.

8. A tomato is classified as a fruit, but most people consider it a vegetable _____ it is prepared and eaten in the same ways as lettuce, onions, and other vegetables.

9. In ancient Rome, garlic was believed to make people courageous Roman soldiers _____ ate large quantities of it before a battle.

PART II: Complete the sentences with *due to, since,* or *consequently*. Add any necessary punctuation and capitalization.

1. _____ his poor eyesight John has to sit in the front row in class.

2. _____ John has poor eyesight he has to sit in the front row.

3. John has poor eyesight _____ he has to sit in the front row.

4. Sarah is afraid of heights _____ she will not walk across a bridge.

5. Sarah will not walk across a bridge _____ her fear of heights.

6. _____ a camel can go completely without water for eight to ten days it is an ideal animal for desert areas.

7. Mark is overweight _____ his doctor has advised him to exercise regularly.

8. _____ a diamond is extremely hard it can be used to cut glass.

9. _____ consumer demand for ivory many African elephants are being slaughtered ruthlessly _____ many people who care about saving these animals from extinction refuse to buy any item made from ivory.

◇ **PRACTICE 22—SELFSTUDY: Using *such . . . that* and *so . . . that*. (Chart 8-10)**

Directions: Add *such* or *so* to the following sentences.

1. The wind was ____**so**____ strong that it blew my hat off my head.

2. Sue is ____**such**____ a good pianist that I'm surprised she didn't go into music professionally.

3. The radio was _____ loud that I couldn't hear what Michael was saying.

4. The food was _____ hot that it burned my tongue.

5. Alison did _____ a poor job that she was fired.

6. Professor James is _____ a stern taskmaster that lazy students won't take his class.

7. The restaurant patron at the table near us was _____ belligerent that we all felt embarrassed, especially when he swept everything off the table and demanded his money back.

8. Small animals in the forest move about _____ quickly that one can barely catch a glimpse of them.

9. The intricate metal lacework on the Eiffel Tower in Paris was _____ complicated that the structure took more than two and a half years to complete.

10. Charles and his brother are _____ hard-working carpenters that I'm sure they'll make a success of their new business.

11. The children had _____ much fun at the carnival that they begged to go again.

12. There are _____ many leaves on a single tree that it is impossible to count them.

13. _____ few students signed up for the course that it was canceled.

14. I feel like I have _____ little energy that I wonder if I'm getting sick.

15. Jan and Arlene have always been _____ good friends that it's a shame to see them not speaking to each other.

16. Indian food can be hot and spicy. Jack ate some very hot chicken curry when he was in India a year ago. In fact, it was _____ hot that smoke came out of his ears!

◇ **PRACTICE 23—GUIDED STUDY: Using *such . . . that* and *so . . . that*. (Chart 8-10)**

Directions: Add *such* or *so*, and complete the sentences with your own words.

Examples:

I'm really fond of my old car, but it's in _____ terrible shape that . . . .
→ *I'm really fond of my old car, but it's in such terrible shape that I'm going to have to get rid of it.*

When the passenger was told that his seat was no longer available on the plane, he became _____ angry that . . . .
→ *When the passenger was told that his seat was no longer available on the plane, he became so angry that he pounded his fist on the counter and threatened to sue the airline.*

1. Larry was _____ exhausted after working for ten straight hours that . . . .

2. I couldn't help it! When Al told me that joke, I laughed _____ hard that . . . .

3. Bill always snores when he sleeps. In fact, he is _____ a loud snorer that . . . .

4. I had been away from home for three years before I was finally able to return for a visit. When I first saw my family at the airport, I felt _____ happy that . . .

5. Sandra was planning to take a long vacation, but her boss suddenly gave her _____ much work to do that . . . .

6. Janet is a travel agent, and she uses her computer for nearly everything in her work. It is _____ an essential piece of equipment that . . . .

7. It was a dangerous situation. _____ many fans crowded together outside the sports arena that . . . .

8. John is the laziest person I've ever met. He is _____ lazy that . . . .

9. My neighbor has six beautiful children who are full of fun and laughter. Sometimes, however,

    they are _____ noisy children that . . . .

10. My sister is the world's worst cook. Her cooking is _____ bad that . . . .

11. . . . _____ exhausted that . . . .

12. . . . _____ a good time that . . . .

13. . . . _____ shy that . . . .

14. . . . _____ many people that . . . .

◇ PRACTICE 24—SELFSTUDY: Using *so that*. (Chart 8-11)

Directions: Complete the sentences in COLUMN A with the ideas in COLUMN B. Pay special attention to the verb forms following *so that*.

Examples:

Column A

1. Ali borrowed an eraser so that . . . .
2. Jack fixed the leak in the boat so that . . . .
3. I need to buy some laundry detergent so that . . . .

Column B

A. wash my clothes
B. erase a mistake in his composition
C. not sink

→ 1. *Ali borrowed an eraser so that **he could erase** a mistake in his composition.*
→ 2. *Jack fixed the leak in the boat so that **it wouldn't sink**.*
→ 3. *I need to buy some laundry detergent so that **I can wash** my clothes.*

Column A

1. I turned up the radio so that . . . .

2. Roberto is studying the history and government of Canada so that . . . .

3. Carolyn put on her reading glasses so that . . . .

4. Jane is taking a course in auto mechanics so that . . . .

5. Al is working hard to impress his supervisor so that . . . .

6. Nancy is carrying extra courses every semester so that . . . .

7. Jason is tired of work and school. He wants to take a semester off so that . . . .

8. Suzanne lowered the volume on the TV set so that . . . .

9. During the parade, James lifted his daughter to his shoulder so that . . . .

10. Whenever we are planning a vacation, we call a travel agent so that . . . .

Column B

A. read the fine print at the bottom of the contract

B. travel in Europe

C. fix her own car

D. see the dancers in the street

E. get expert advice on our itinerary

F. not disturb her roommate

G. listen to the news

H. be considered for a promotion at this company

I. become a Canadian citizen

J. graduate early

◇ **PRACTICE 25—GUIDED STUDY: Using *so that*. (Chart 8-11)**

Directions: Complete the sentences with your own words.

Examples:
    Sam took lots of pictures on his vacation so (that) . . . .
    → *Sam took lots of pictures on his vacation so (that) he could show his family where he had been.*

    . . . so (that) I could see better.
    → *I moved to the front of the room so (that) I could see better.*

1. I need a pen so (that) . . . .
2. . . . so (that) he can improve his English.
3. I turned on the TV so (that) . . . .
4. Mary hurried to get the child out of the road so (that) . . . .
5. . . . so (that) he wouldn't miss his important appointment.
6. I'm taking a bus instead of flying so (that) . . . .
7. . . . so (that) I could tell him the news in person.
8. . . . so (that) his children will have a better life.
9. Martina is trying to improve her English so (that) . . . .
10. . . . so (that) the celebration would be a great success.
11. Ralph borrowed some money from his friend so (that) . . . .
12. . . . so (that) you can be ready to leave on time.

◇ **PRACTICE 26—GUIDED STUDY: Cause and effect. (Charts 8-1, 8-4, 8-6 → 8-11)**

Directions: Choose **ALL** of the correct completions for each sentence. There may be more than one correct completion.

Example:
    _____ **A, C, D** _____ *I was tired, I went to bed.*
    A. *Because*   B. *For*   C. *Since*   D. *Due to the fact that*

1. A small fish needs camouflage to hide itself _____ its enemies cannot find it.
    A. so that   B. so   C. therefore   D. due to

2. Josh couldn't open the door _____ the lock was broken.
    A. because   B. therefore   C. so   D. due to the fact that

3. The workers have gone on strike. _____, all production has ceased.
    A. Because   B. Therefore   C. Consequently   D. Inasmuch as

4. _____ my company's bid for building the library was the lowest, we were awarded the contract.
    A. Because   B. Since   C. For   D. Inasmuch as

5. I needed to finish the marathon race _____ I could prove that I had the strength and stamina to do it. I didn't care whether I won or not.
    A. because of   B. so that   C. for   D. therefore

6. Let's ask our teacher how to solve this problem _____ we can't agree on the answer.
    A. since   B. because of   C. consequently   D. as long as

7. Our apartment building has had two robberies in the last month, _____ I'm going to put an extra lock on the door and install a telephone in my bedroom.
   A. now that   B. so that   C. so   D. since

8. The Chippewas are Native North Americans. Their language is one of the most complex in the world, _____ it contains more than 6,000 verb forms.
   A. consequently   B. so   C. so that   D. for

9. _____ the bad grease stain on the carpet, we had to rearrange the furniture before the company arrived.
   A. Because of   B. Now that   C. Due to   D. Since

10. The price of airline tickets has gone down recently. _____ the tickets cost less, more people are flying than before.
    A. Consequently   B. Because of   C. Because   D. For

11. The mountain road was closed to all traffic _____ the heavy rainfall had caused a huge mudslide that blocked the way.
    A. therefore   B. because   C. due to   D. so

12. Janet called the security guard _____ someone had taken her briefcase while she was making a call at the public phone.
    A. so that   B. so   C. because   D. because of

13. Dolphins are sometimes caught and killed in commercial fishing nets _____ they often swim in schools with other fish, such as tuna.
    A. since   B. as   C. so   D. because

14. We can finally afford to trade in the old car for a new one _____ I've gotten the raise I've been waiting for.
    A. so that   B. now that   C. consequently   D. so

◇ **PRACTICE 27—SELFSTUDY: Reduction of adverb clauses to modifying phrases. (Charts 8-12 and 8-13)**

Directions: Change the adverb clause to a modifying phrase.

          opening
1. Since ~~he opened~~ his new business, Bob has been working 16 hours a day.

          leaving
2. I shut off the lights before ~~I left~~ the room.

3. While he was herding his goats in the mountains, an Ethiopian named Kaldi discovered the coffee plant more than 1200 years ago.

4. Before they marched into battle, ancient Ethiopian soldiers ate a mixture of raw coffee beans and fat for extra energy.

5. After I had met the movie star in person, I understood why she was so popular.

6. I found my keys after I searched through all my pockets.

7. When it was first brought to Europe, the tomato was thought to be poisonous.

8. Since it was first imported into Australia many years ago, the rabbit has become a serious pest because it has no natural enemies there.

◇ PRACTICE 28—SELFSTUDY: Modifying phrases. (Chart 8-13)

Directions: Underline the subject of the adverb clause and the subject of the main clause. Change the adverb clauses to modifying phrases if possible.

1. After the musician stopped playing, the audience stood and clapped enthusiastically.
   → (no change possible)

2. After the police stopped the fight, they arrested two men and a woman.
   → After stopping the fight, the police arrested two men and a woman.

3. Since Bob opened his new business, he has been working 16 hours a day.
   → Since opening his new business, Bob has been working 16 hours a day.

4. While Sam was driving to work in the rain, his car got a flat tire.

5. While Sam was driving to work, he had a flat tire.

6. Before Paulo returned to his country, his American friends gave him a surprise going-away party.

7. Since the Irish immigrated to the United States in large numbers in the mid-1800s, Americans have celebrated Halloween and St. Patrick's Day as holidays.

8. After Tom had worked hard in the garden all afternoon, he took a shower and then went to the movies with his friends.

9. Before a friend tries to do something hard, an American may say "Break a leg!" to wish him or her good luck.

10. Before George took his driving test, the police officer asked him a few questions about the traffic laws.

11. After Sunita had made a delicious chicken curry for her friends, they wanted the recipe.

12. Emily always straightens her desk before she leaves the office at the end of the day.

13. Before Nick left on his trip, his boss gave him a big raise.

◇ PRACTICE 29—SELFSTUDY: Reduction of adverb clauses to modifying phrases. (Charts 8-12 and 8-13)

Directions: Complete the sentences with the correct forms of the verbs in parentheses.

1. a. Before (leave) ___*leaving*___ on his trip, Tom renewed his passport.
   b. Before Tom (leave) ___*left*___ on his trip, he renewed his passport.

2. a. After Thomas Edison (invent) ___*invented/had invented*___ the light bulb, he went on to create many other useful inventions.
   b. After (invent) ___*inventing/having invented*___ the light bulb, Thomas Edison went on to create many other useful inventions.

3. a. While (work) _____ with uranium ore, Marie Curie discovered two new elements, radium and polonium.
   b. While she (work) _____ with uranium ore, Marie Curie discovered two new elements, radium and polonium.

4. a. Before an astronaut (fly) _____ on a space mission, s/he will have undergone thousands of hours of training.
   b. Before (fly) _____ on a space mission, an astronaut will have undergone thousands of hours of training.

5. a. After they (*study*) _____ the stars, the ancient Mayans in Central America developed a very accurate solar calendar.

 b. After (*study*) _____ the stars, the ancient Mayans in Central America developed a very accurate solar calendar.

6. a. Since (*learn*) _____ that cigarettes cause cancer, many people have stopped smoking.

 b. Since they (*learn*) _____ that cigarettes cause cancer, many people have stopped smoking.

7. a. Aspirin can be poisonous when it (*take*) _____ in excessive amounts.

 b. Aspirin can be poisonous when (*take*) _____ in excessive amounts.

8. a. When (*take*) _____ aspirin, you should be sure to follow the directions on the bottle.

 b. When you (*take*) _____ aspirin, you should be sure to follow the directions on the bottle.

9. a. I took a wrong turn while I (*drive*) _____ to my uncle's house and ended up back where I started.

 b. I took a wrong turn while (*drive*) _____ to my uncle's house and ended up back where I started.

◇ **PRACTICE 30—SELFSTUDY: Modifying phrases. (Charts 8-14 and 8-15)**

Directions: Combine the two sentences, making a modifying phrase out of the first sentence, *if possible*.

1. Anna kept one hand on the steering wheel. She opened a can of soda pop with her free hand.
 → ***Keeping*** *one hand on the steering wheel,* ***Anna*** *opened a can of soda pop with her free hand.*

2. Anna kept one hand on the steering wheel. Bob handed her a can of pop to hold in the other hand. → (*no change possible*)

3. I misunderstood the directions to the hotel. I arrived one hour late for the dinner party.

4. I misunderstood the directions to the hotel. The taxi driver didn't know how to get there either.

5. The taxi driver misunderstood my directions to the hotel. He took me to the wrong place.

6. I live a long distance from my work. I have to commute daily by train.

7. Heidi lives a long distance from her work. She has to commute daily by train.

8. Fred lives a long distance from his work. His car is essential.

9. Martha was picking strawberries in the garden. A bumblebee stung her.

10. Ann remembered that she hadn't turned off the oven. She went directly home.

11. Jim tripped on the carpet. He spilt his coffee.

12. I recognized his face but I had forgotten his name. I just smiled and said, "Hi."

13. We slowly approached the door to the hospital. The nurse stepped out to greet us.

14. I was lying by the swimming pool. I realized I was getting sunburned.

15. I met Gina after work. She suggested playing tennis.

16. My family and I live in the Pacific Northwest, where it rains a great deal. We are accustomed to cool, damp weather.

Directions: Make sentences that combine a modifying phrase with a main clause. Write the capital letter of the most logical main clause to complete the sentence. Use each capital letter only one time.

Modifying phrases:

1. Trying to understand the physics problem, __*E*__

2. Since injuring my arm, _____

3. Fighting for her life, _____

4. Wanting to ask a question, _____

5. Exhausted after washing the windows, _____

6. Not wanting to disturb the manager, _____

7. Upon hearing the announcement that their plane was delayed, _____

8. Talking with the employees after work, _____

9. Attempting to enter the freeway, _____

10. Currently selling at record-low prices, _____

11. Stepping onto the platform to receive their medals, _____

12. Before turning in your exam paper, _____

Main clauses:

A. the desperate woman grasped a floating log after the boat capsized.

B. I collapsed in my chair for a rest.

C. the taxi driver caused a multiple-car accident.

D. carefully proofread all your answers.

✔ E. the students repeated the experiment.

F. the athletes waved to the cheering crowd.

G. the little girl raised her hand.

H. the manager learned of their dissatisfaction with their jobs.

I. the passengers angrily walked back to the ticket counter.

J. I haven't been able to play tennis.

K. gold is considered a good investment.

L. the worker in charge of Section B of the assembly line told the assistant manager about the problem.

◇ PRACTICE 32—GUIDED STUDY: Modifying phrases. (Charts 8-14 and 8-15)

Directions: Make sentences by combining the ideas in Column A and Column B. Use the idea in Column A as a modifying phrase. Show logical relationships.

Examples:

Column A	**Column B**
1. She was looking in the want ads in the Sunday newspaper.	A. Mary has a lot of responsibilities.
2. She had grown up overseas.	B. Ann found a good used car at a price she could afford to pay.
3. She is the vice president of a large company.	C. Alice enjoys trying foods from other countries.

→ 1. *Looking in the want ads in the Sunday newspaper, Ann found a used car for a good price.*
→ 2. *Having grown up overseas, Alice enjoys trying foods from other countries.*
→ 3. *Being the vice-president of a large company, Mary has a lot of responsibilities.*

Column A	**Column B**
1. They have sticky pads on their feet.	A. Sally didn't know what to expect when she went to the Thai restaurant for dinner.
2. He has worked with computers for many years	B. Mice can hide in almost any part of a house.
3. She was born two months prematurely.	C. Rhinos are protected by law from poachers who kill them solely for their horns.
4. He had done everything he could for the patient.	D. The doctor left to attend to other people.
5. She had never eaten Thai food before.	E. Nancy expects to be hired by a top company after graduation.
6. He had no one to turn to for help.	F. Diamonds are used extensively in industry to cut other hard minerals.
7. They are an endangered species.	G. Flies can easily walk on the ceiling.
8. They are able to crawl into very small spaces.	H. Sam was forced to work out the problem by himself.
9. She has done very well in her studies and is finally nearly finished.	I. Mary needed special care for the first few days of her life.
10. They are extremely hard and nearly indestructible.	J. Robert has an excellent understanding of their limitations as well as their potential.

◇ PRACTICE 33—SELFSTUDY: Modifying phrases with *upon*. (Chart 8-16)

Directions: Write completions using the ideas in the italicized sentences.

I heard my name called.
✔ *I arrived at the airport.*
She learned the problem was not at all serious.
She was told she got it.

He investigated the cause.
He heard those words.
He discovered it was hot.
I reached the other side of the lake.

1. It had been a long, uncomfortable trip. Upon _____ ***arriving at the airport*** _____, I

quickly unfastened my seatbelt and stood in the aisle waiting my turn to disembark.

2. I rented a small fishing boat last weekend, but I ended up doing more rowing than I did fishing. The motor died halfway across the lake, so I had to row to shore. It was a long distance away. Upon _____, I was exhausted.

3. The small child reached toward the lighted candle. Upon _____

_____, he jerked his hand back, held it in front of himself, and stared at it curiously. Then he began to scream.

4. There must have been over 300 students in the room on the first day of class. The professor slowly read through the list of names. Upon _____, I raised my hand to identify myself.

5. Captain Cook had been sailing for many weeks with no land in sight. Finally, one of the sailors shouted, "Land ahoy!" Upon _____, Cook grabbed his telescope and searched the horizon.

6. At first, we thought the fire had been caused by lightning. However, upon _____

_____, the fire chief determined it had been caused by faulty electrical wiring.

7. Amy felt terrible. She was sure she had some dread disease, so she went to her doctor for some tests. Upon _____, she was extremely relieved.

8. Janet wanted that scholarship with all her heart and soul. Upon _____

_____, she jumped straight up in the air and let out a scream of happiness.

◇ PRACTICE 34—SELFSTUDY: Modifying phrases. (Charts 8-13 → 8-16)

Directions: Change the adverb clause in each sentence to an adverb phrase *if possible.* Make any necessary changes in punctuation, capitalization, or word order.

1. After it spends some time in a cocoon, a caterpillar will emerge as a butterfly.
   → *After spending some time in a cocoon, a caterpillar will emerge as a butterfly.*

2. When the movie started, the audience suddenly got very quiet.
   → *(no change possible)*

3. When we entered the theater, we handed the usher our tickets.
   → *Upon entering the theater, we handed the usher our tickets.*

4. Because I was unprepared for the test, I didn't do well.
   → *Being unprepared for the test, I didn't do well.* OR: *Unprepared for the test, I didn't do well.*

5. Before I left on my trip, I checked to see what shots I would need.

6. Since Indians in the high Andes Mountains live in thin air, their hearts grow to be a larger than average size.

7. Because I hadn't understood the directions, I got lost.

8. My father reluctantly agreed to let me attend the game after he had talked it over with my mother.

9. When I discovered I had lost my key to the apartment, I called the building supervisor.

10. Jane's family hasn't received any news from her since she arrived in Australia two weeks ago.

11. Garcia Lopez de Cardenas accidentally discovered the Grand Canyon while he was looking for the legendary Lost City of Gold.

12. Because the forest area is so dry this summer, it is prohibited to light camp fires.

13. After we had to wait for over half an hour, we were finally seated at the restaurant.

14. Before Maria got accepted on her country's Olympic running team, she had spent most of the two previous years in training.

15. Because George wasn't paying attention to his driving, he didn't see the large truck until it was almost too late.

◇ PRACTICE 35—GUIDED STUDY: Modifying phrases. (Charts 8-13 → 8-16)

Directions: Underline the adverb clauses in the following. Change the adverb clauses to adverb phrases *if possible*. Make any necessary changes in punctuation, capitalization, or word order.

1. Alexander Graham Bell, a teacher of the deaf in Boston, invented the first telephone. One day in 1875, while he was running a test on his latest attempt to create a machine that could carry voices, he accidentally spilled acid on his coat. Naturally, he called for his assistant, Thomas A. Watson, who was in another room. Bell said, "Mr. Watson, come here. I want you." When Watson heard words coming from the machine, he immediately realized that their experiments had at last been successful. He rushed excitedly into the other room to tell Bell that he had heard his words over the machine.

   After Bell had successfully tested the new apparatus again and again, he confidently announced his invention to the world. For the most part, scientists appreciated his accomplishment, but the general public did not understand the revolutionary nature of Bell's invention. Because they believed the telephone was a toy with little practical application, most people paid little attention to Bell's announcement.

2. Wolves are much misunderstood animals. Because many people believe that wolves eagerly kill human beings, they fear them. However, the truth is that wolves eagerly avoid any contact with human beings. U.S. wildlife biologists say there is no documented case of wolves attacking humans in the lower 48 states. More people are hurt and killed by buffaloes in Yellowstone Park than have ever been hurt by wolves in North America.

   Because they are strictly carnivorous, wolves hunt large animals, such as elk and deer, and small animals, such as mice and rabbits. However, wolves are also particularly fond of sheep. Their killing ranchers' livestock has helped lead to their bad reputation among people.

   Because it was relentlessly poisoned, trapped, and shot by ranchers and hunters, the timber wolf, a subspecies of the gray wolf, was eradicated in the lower 48 by the 1940s. Not one wolf remained. In the 1970s, because they realized a mistake had been made, U.S. lawmakers passed laws to protect wolves.

Long ago, wolves could be found in almost all areas of the Northern Hemisphere throughout Asia, Europe, and North America. Today, after they have been unremittingly destroyed for centuries, they are found in few places, principally in sparsely populated areas of Alaska, Minnesota, Canada, and the northernmost regions of Russia and China.

◇ **PRACTICE 36—SELFSTUDY: Error analysis: modifying phrases. (Charts 8-13→8-16)**

Directions: Write ''I'' if the sentence is INCORRECT. Write ''C'' if the sentence is CORRECT. Reminder: A modifying phrase must modify the subject of the sentence.

1. __*I*__ While taking a trip across Europe this summer, Jane's camera suddenly quit working.

2. __*C*__ When using a microwave oven for the first time, read the instructions carefully about the kind of dish you can use.

3. _____ Having been given their instructions, the teacher told her students to begin working on the test.

4. _____ After receiving the Nobel Peace Prize in 1979, Mother Teresa returned to Calcutta, India, to work and live among the poor, the sick, and the dying.

5. _____ Having studied Greek for several years, Sarah's pronunciation was easy to understand.

6. _____ Since returning to her country after graduation, Maria's parents have enjoyed having all their children home again.

7. _____ While bicycling across the United States, the wheels on my bike had to be replaced several times.

8. _____ Not wanting to interrupt the conversation, I stood quietly and listened until I could have a chance to talk.

9. _____ Being too young to understand death, my mother gave me a simple explanation of where my grandfather had gone.

10. _____ When asked to explain his mistake, the new employee cleared his throat nervously.

11. _____ While working in my office late last night, someone suddenly knocked loudly at my door and nearly scared me to death!

12. _____ After hurrying to get everything ready for the picnic, it began to rain just as we were leaving.

13. _____ When told he would have to have surgery, the doctor reassured Bob that he wouldn't have to miss more than a week of work.

14. _____ While walking across the street at a busy intersection, a truck nearly ran over my foot.

15. _____ Before driving across a desert, be sure that your car has good tires as well as enough oil, water, and gas to last the trip.

◇ PRACTICE 37—SELFSTUDY: Error analysis. (Chapter 8)

Directions: Find and correct the errors in the following sentences.

1. I was very tired, go to bed.
   → *I was very tired, so I went to bed.* OR: *I was very tired and went to bed.*

2. Because our leader could not attend the meeting, so it was canceled.

3. I and my wife likes to travel.

4. I always fasten my seatbelt before to start the engine.

5. I don't like our classroom. Because it is hot and crowded. I hope we can change to a different room.

6. The day was very warm and humid, for that I turned on the air conditioner.

7. Upon I learned that my car couldn't be repaired for three days, I am very distressed.

8. Having missed the final examination, the teacher gave me a failing grade.

9. Both my sister and my brother is going to be at the family reunion.

10. I hope my son will remain in school until he will finish his degree.

11. My brother has succeeded in business because of he works hard.

12. Luis stood up, turned toward me, and speaking so softly that I couldn't hear what he said.

13. I was lost. I could not find my parents neither my brother.

14. When I traveled through Europe I visited England, France, Italy, Germany, and Swiss.

◇ PRACTICE 38—GUIDED STUDY: Speaking

Directions: Pair up with another student and make up a short skit (i.e., a very short drama) that demonstrates one of the following emotions. Using both words and gestures, present your skit to the class and ask them to guess the emotion you intended to demonstrate by your skit.

1. anger	7. fear	13. disgust
2. cheerfulness	8. amusement	14. belligerence
3. sadness	9. envy	15. disappointment
4. weariness	10. impatience	16. nervousness
5. embarrassment	11. surprise	17. bewilderment
6. enthusiasm	12. delight	18. boredom

◇ PRACTICE 39—GUIDED STUDY: Writing

Directions: Using one of the following topics, try to communicate in writing an emotion you have felt. Describe the situation that caused this emotion, your actions (and those of any other people who were involved), and your feelings.

1. Describe an occasion when you felt nervous.
2. Describe an occasion when you experienced fear.
3. Describe a time when you felt completely at peace.
4. Describe an occasion when you worried needlessly.
5. Describe a time when you felt very surprised.

◇ PRACTICE TEST A—SELFSTUDY: Showing relationships between ideas. (Chapter 8)

Directions: Choose the correct answer.

Example:
____*B*____ *I get angry and upset, I try to take ten deep breaths.*
  A. *Until*   B. *Whenever*   C. *Therefore*   D. *For*

1. _____ Paul brings the money for our lunch, we'll go right down to the cafeteria.
  A. Since   B. As soon as   C. Now that   D. Until

2. My mouth is burning! This is _____ spicy food that I don't think I can finish it.
  A. such   B. so   C. very   D. too

3. Both my books _____ from my room last night.
  A. were stolen and my wallet   B. and my wallet were stolen
  C. and my wallet was stolen   D. were and my wallet was stolen

4. When _____ a dictionary, you need to be able to understand the symbols and abbreviations it contains.
  A. having used   B. use   C. to use   D. using

5. Bats are fascinating _____ have many interesting and amazing qualities.
  A. animals. Therefore, they   B. animals, they
  C. animals. They   D. animals. Because they

6. While _____ to help Tim with his math, I got impatient because he wouldn't pay attention to what I was saying.
  A. I am trying   B. having tried   C. I try   D. trying

7. _____ extremely bad weather in the mountains, we're no longer considering our skiing trip.
   A. Due to   B. Because   C. Since   D. Due to the fact that

8. Emily is motivated to study _____ she knows that a good education can improve her life.
   A. therefore   B. because of   C. because   D. so

9. Sonia broke her leg in two places. _____, she had to wear a cast and use crutches for three months.
   A. Inasmuch as   B. Consequently   C. For that   D. Because

10. Our village had _____ money available for education that the schools had to close.
    A. so little   B. such little   C. so much   D. such much

11. Hundreds of species of Hawaiian flowers have become extinct or rare _____ land development and the grazing of wild goats.
    A. now that   B. due to   C. because   D. for

12. Tom Booth is one of the best players in the country. We have won all of our games _____ he joined our team.
    A. when   B. the first time   C. since   D. due to

13. Joe seemed to be in a good mood, _____ he snapped at me angrily when I asked him to join us.
    A. yet   B. so   C. for   D. and

14. _____ Jan arrives, we will have finished this group project.
    A. By the time   B. Until   C. Now that   D. Since

15. For the most part, young children spend their time playing, eating, and _____ a lot.
    A. they sleep   B. sleeping   C. sleep   D. they are sleeping

16. Joan worked in a vineyard last summer _____ money for school expenses.
    A. because to earn   B. so she earns
    C. for she earned   D. so that she could earn

17. _____ unprepared for the exam, I felt sure I would get a low score.
    A. Being   B. Having   C. Because   D. Upon

18. Ever since _____ Ted the bad news, he's been avoiding me.
    A. telling   B. told   C. I told   D. having told

19. _____ my daughter reaches the age of sixteen, she will be able to drive.
    A. Having   B. Since   C. Once   D. Because

20. Matt will enjoy skiing more the next time he goes to Mt. Baker _____ he has had skiing lessons.
    A. so that   B. before   C. now that   D. and

◇ **PRACTICE TEST B—GUIDED STUDY: Showing relationships between ideas. (Chapter 8)**

Directions: Choose the correct answer.

Example:
   __*B*__ *I get angry and upset, I try to take ten deep breaths.*
   A. Until   B. Whenever   C. Therefore   D. For

1. _____ it's warm and sunny today, why don't we go to the park?
   A. Therefore   B. Due to   C. As long as   D. For

2. The first time I went swimming in deep water, I sank to the bottom like a rock. _____ I've learned to stay afloat, I feel better about the water, but I still can't swim well.
   A. As soon as   B. The first time   C. When   D. Now that

3. It's obvious that neither the workers _____ to fight the new rules.
   A. nor the manager intend   B. intend nor the manager
   C. nor the manager intends   D. intend nor the manager intends

4. Timmy doesn't do well in school _____ his inability to concentrate on any one thing for longer than a minute or two.
    A. as   B. due to   C. because   D. therefore

5. After _____ to 45 minutes of an extremely boring speech, I found myself nodding off.
    A. was listening   B. listen   C. listening   D. having listen

6. Why did I stay until the end? I am never going to stay and watch a bad movie again! _____ I am in that situation, I'm going to leave the theater immediately.
    A. The next time   B. Now that   C. After   D. Until

7. "Why aren't you ready to go?"
   "I am ready."
   "How can that be? It's freezing outside, _____ you're wearing shorts and a T-shirt!"
    A. for   B. so   C. because   D. yet

8. Erin likes to swim, jog, and _____ tennis.
    A. plays   B. play   C. to play   D. playing

9. Since _____ to a warmer and less humid climate, I've had no trouble with my asthma.
    A. upon moving   B. I moving   C. moving   D. I move

10. Tony spent _____ money buying movie tickets that he didn't have enought left to buy a soft drink or candy bar.
    A. such   B. a lot of   C. too much   D. so much

11. _____ I get back from my next business trip, I'm taking a few days off. I'm worn out!
    A. Once   B. Since   C. Now that   D. Every time

12. Citrus growers become anxious about losing their fragile crop of oranges _____ the temperature gets near freezing in Florida.
    A. and   B. consequently   C. until   D. whenever

13. Before _____ a promotion and transfer to another city, I will discuss it at length with my whole family to be sure that everyone will be able to adjust to the change.
    A. accept   B. accepted
    C. having been accepted   D. accepting

14. You should learn how to change a tire on your car _____ you can handle an emergency situation if necessary.
    A. so that   B. when   C. for that   D. therefore

15. Cars have become much more complicated. _____, mechanics need more training than in the past.
    A. Because   B. Therefore   C. So that   D. For

16. Not wanting to be late my first day of class, _____ to school after I missed my bus.
    A. so I ran   B. because I ran   C. I ran   D. therefore, I ran

17. It was raining _____ I couldn't go outside.
    A. because   B. so hard that   C. so that   D. too hard that

18. The Northern Hemisphere has mostly westerly winds _____ the rotation of the earth toward the east.
    A. due to   B. because   C. therefore   D. so

19. Great white sharks are dangerous to _____ will attack without warning.
    A. humans, they   B. humans
    C. humans. Because they   D. humans. They

20. _____ the need to finish this project soon, I want you to work on this overtime for the next few days.
    A. Because   B. So that   C. Because of   D. Inasmuch as

CHAPTER 9
Showing Relationships Between Ideas—Part II

◇ **PRACTICE 1—SELFSTUDY:** Using *even though* vs. *because.* (Chart 9-1)

Directions: Complete the sentences with *even though* or *because*.

1. I put on my sunglasses _____ **even though** _____ it was a dark, cloudy day.

2. I put on my sunglasses _____ **because** _____ the sun was bright.

3. _____ she has a job, she doesn't make enough money to support her four

   children.

4. _____ she has a job, she is able to pay her rent and provide food for her

   family.

5. I'm going horseback riding with Judy this afternoon _____ I'm afraid of

   horses.

6. I'm going horseback riding with Judy this afternoon _____ I enjoy it.

7. _____ you've made it clear that you don't want any help, I have to at

   least offer to help you.

8. I knew that I should get some sleep, but I just couldn't put my book down _____

   I was really enjoying it.

9. I'm glad that my mother made me take piano lessons when I was a child _____

   I hated it at the time. Now, I play the piano every day.

10. _____ Tom didn't know how to dance, he wanted to go to the school

    dance _____ he felt lonely sitting and staring blankly at the TV while all

    of his friends were having fun together.

11. Joe jumped into the river to rescue the little girl who was drowning _____ he wasn't a

    good swimmer.

12. My hair stylist subscribes to three different fashion magazines _____

    she's not interested in clothes. She subscribes to them _____ her customers

    like them.

13. _____ the earthquake damaged the bridge across Skunk River, the

    Smiths were able to cross the river _____ they had a boat.

◇ PRACTICE 2—GUIDED STUDY: Using *even though* vs. *because*. (Chart 9-1)

Directions: Write sentences that include the given words. Use any tense or modal for the verb in parentheses.

Examples:

Because _____, I (*walk*) _____ all the way home.
→ *Because the bus drivers went on strike, I had to walk all the way home.*

Even though _____, I (*walk*) _____ all the way home.
→ *Even though I was dead tired, I walked all the way home.*

1. Because _____, I (*go*) _____ fishing.

2. Even though _____, I (*go*) _____ fishing.

3. I (*pay*) _____ for everyone's dinner because _____

4. I (*pay*) _____ for everyone's dinner even though _____

5. Even though there (*be*) _____ very few customers in the store, _____

6. Because there (*be*) _____ very few customers in the store, _____

7. I (*wear*) _____ heavy gloves because _____

8. Even though my feet (*be*) _____ killing me and my head (*be*) _____ pounding, I _____

9. Even though _____, I (*get, not*) _____ a traffic ticket.

10. Even though I (*ask*) _____ him politely to speak more softly, _____

11. My friend (*subscribe*) _____ to three different fashion magazines because

_____

12. When I (*open*) _____ the door, my roommate (*scream*)_____ because

_____

13. Even though I (*be*) _____ tired, I _____ because _____

14. Even though _____ when _____, I _____ because

_____

15. Because _____ while _____, I _____ even though

_____

◇ PRACTICE 3—SELFSTUDY: Showing opposition. (Chart 9-2)

Directions: Complete the sentences with the given words. Pay close attention to the given punctuation and capitalization.

PART I: Complete the following with *but, even though,* or *nevertheless*.

1. Bob ate a large dinner. _____ ***Nevertheless*** _____, he is still hungry.

2. Bob ate a large dinner, _____ ***but*** _____ he is still hungry.

3. Bob is still hungry _____ ***even though*** _____ he ate a large dinner.

4. I had a lot of studying to do, _____ I went to a movie anyway.

5. I had a lot of studying to do. _____, I went to a movie.

6. _____ I had a lot of studying to do, I went to a movie.

7. I finished all of my work _____ I was very sleepy.

8. I was very sleepy, _____ I finished all of my work anyway.

9. I was very sleepy. _____, I finished all of my work.

10. All of my family friends have advised me not to travel abroad during this time of political
    turmoil. _____, I'm leaving next week to begin a trip around the world.

PART II: Complete the following sentences with **yet, although,** or **however.**

11. I washed my hands. _____, they still looked dirty.

12. I washed my hands, _____ they still looked dirty.

13. _____ I washed my hands, they still looked dirty.

14. Diana didn't know how to swim, _____ she jumped into the swimming pool.

15. _____ Diana didn't know how to swim, she jumped into the swimming pool.

16. Diana didn't know how to swim. _____, she jumped into the swimming pool.

17. I wouldn't trust Alan with my money _____ he seems to be trustworthy.

18. Alan seems trustworthy and capable as a financial advisor, _____ I
    wouldn't trust him with my money.

19. Alan seems capable as a financial advisor. _____, i wouldn't trust him
    with my money.

20. Some people think great strides have been made in cleaning up the environment in much of
    the world. _____, others think the situation is much worse than it was
    twenty years ago.

◇ **PRACTICE 4—SELFSTUDY: Showing opposition: punctuation. (Chart 9-2)**

Directions: Add commas, periods, and capital letters as necessary. Do not add or omit any words.
Do not change the order of the words.

1. Anna's father gave her some good advice nevertheless she did not follow it.
   → *Anna's father gave her some good advice. Nevertheless, she did not follow it.*

2. Anna's father gave her some good advice but she didn't follow it.

3. Even though Anna's father gave her some good advice she didn't follow it.

4. Anna's father gave her some good advice she did not follow it however.

5. Thomas was thirsty I offered him some water he refused it.

6. Thomas refused the water although he was thirsty.

7. Thomas was thirsty he nevertheless refused the glass of water I brought him.

8. Thomas was thirsty yet he refused to drink the water that I offered him.

◇ **PRACTICE 5—SELFSTUDY:** *Despite/in spite of* vs. *even though/although.* (Chart 9-2)

Directions: Choose the correct completions.

1. a. *(Even though)* *Despite* her doctor warned her, Carol has continued to smoke nearly three packs of cigarettes a day.

   b. *Even though,* *(Despite)* her doctor's warnings, Carol has continued to smoke nearly three packs of cigarettes a day.

   c. *Even though,* *(Despite)* the warnings her doctor gave her, Carol continues to smoke.

   d. *Even though,* *(Despite)* the fact that her doctor warned her of dangers to her health, Carol continues to smoke.

   e. *(Even though)* *Despite* she has been warned about the dangers of smoking by her doctor, Carol continues to smoke.

2. a. *Although, In spite of* an approaching storm, the two climbers continued their trek up the mountain.

   b. *Although, In spite of* a storm was approaching, the two climbers continued their trek.

   c. *Although, In spite of* there was an approaching storm, the two climbers continued up the mountain.

   d. *Although, In spite of* the storm that was approaching the mountain area, the two climbers continued their trek.

   e. *Although, in spite of* the fact that a storm was approaching the mountain area, the two climbers continued their trek.

3. a. *Although, Despite* his many hours of practice, George failed his driving test for the third time.

   b. *Although, Despite* he had practiced for many hours, George failed his driving test for the third time.

   c. *Although, Despite* practicing for many hours, George failed his driving test again.

   d. *Although, Despite* his mother and father spent hours with him in the car trying to teach him how to drive, George failed his driving test repeatedly.

   e. *Although, Despite* his mother and father's efforts to teach him how to drive, George failed his driving test.

4. a. *Even though, In spite of*   repeated crop failures due to drought, the villagers are refusing to leave their traditional homeland for resettlement in other areas.

   b. *Even though, In spite of*   their crops have failed repeatedly due to drought, the villagers are refusing to leave their traditional homeland for resettlement in other areas.

   c. The villagers refused to leave   *even though, in spite of*   the drought.

   d. The villagers refuse to leave   *even though, in spite of*   the drought seriously threatens their food supply.

   e. The villagers refuse to leave   *even though, in spite of*   the threat to their food supply because of the continued drought.

   f. The villagers refuse to leave   *even though, in spite of*   the threat to their food supply is serious because of the continued drought.

   g. The villagers refuse to leave   *even though, in spite of*   their food supply is threatened.

   h. The villagers refused to leave   *even though, in spite of*   their threatened food supply.

◇ **PRACTICE 6—SELFSTUDY:** Using *in spite of/despite,* and *even though/though/although.* (Chart 9-2)

Directions: Complete the sentences. Place the letter of the completion in the blank space. Use each completion only one time.

   A. *its many benefits*
 ✔ B. *its inherent dangers*
   C. *it has been shown to be safe*
   D. *it has been shown to cause birth defects and sometimes death*
   E. *his fear of heights*
   F. *he is afraid of heights*
   G. *he is normally quite shy and sometimes inarticulate*
   H. *an inability to communicate well in any language besides English*
   I. *having excellent skills in the job category they were trying to fill*
   J. *he had the necessary qualifications*

1. In spite of ___**B**___, nuclear energy is a clean and potentially inexhaustible source of energy.

2. In spite of _____, Carl enjoyed his helicopter trip over the Grand Canyon in Arizona.

3. Because of his age, John was not hired even though _____.

4. Although _____, Mark rode an elevator to the top of the World Trade Center in New York for the magnificent view.

5. Although _____, many people avoid using a microwave oven for fear of its rays.

6. Jack usually has little trouble making new friends in another country despite _____.

7. In spite of _____, the use of chemotherapy to treat cancer has many severe side effects.

8. Though _____, Bob managed to give an excellent presentation at the board meeting.

9. Jerry continued to be denied a promotion despite _____.

10. DDT is still used in many countries as a primary insecticide even though _____.

◇ PRACTICE 7—SELFSTUDY: Direct opposition. (Chart 9-3)

Directions: Choose the best completion.

1. Some people are tall, whereas others are ___C___.
   A. intelligent   B. thin
   C. short   D. large

2. A box is square, whereas _____.
   A. a rectangle has four sides   B. my village has a town square in the center
   C. we use envelopes for letters   D. a circle is round

3. While some parts of the world get an abundance of rain, others _____.
   A. are warm and humid   B. are cold and wet
   C. get little or none   D. get a lot

4. In some nations coffee is the favorite beverage, while _____.
   A. I like tea   B. it has caffeine
   C. in others it is tea   D. tea has caffeine too.

5. Some people like cream and sugar in their coffee, while _____.
   A. others drink hot coffee   B. others like it black
   C. milk is good in coffee, too   D. sugar can cause cavities

6. Jack is an interesting storyteller and conversationalist. His brother, on the other hand, _____.
   A. is a newspaper reporter.   B. bores other people by talking about himself
   C. has four children   D. knows a lot of stories, too

◇ PRACTICE 8—GUIDED STUDY: Direct opposition. (Chart 9-3)

Directions: Complete the sentences with your own words.

1. Some people really enjoy swimming, while others . . . *are afraid of water.*

2. In the U.S., people drive on the righthand side of the road. However, people in . . . .

3. While my apartment always seems to be a mess, my . . . .

4. Marge keeps to herself and has few friends. Carol, on the other hand, ...

5. People who grew up on farms are accustomed to dealing with various kinds of animals. However, city people like myself . . . .

6. Teak is a hard wood that is difficult to cut. Balsa, on the other hand, ...

7. My oldest son is shy, while my youngest son . . . .

8. I'm righthanded. That means that I can accomplish difficult manipulations with my right hand. However, ...

◇ PRACTICE 9—SELFSTUDY: Cause/effect and opposition. (Charts 8-6 → 8-9 and 9-1 → 9-3)

Directions: Choose the best completion.

Example:
   It was cold and wet. ___D___, *Bob put on his swimming suit and went to the beach.*
      A. Therefore   *B. Despite*   *C. Although*   *D. Nevertheless*

1. I can't ride my bicycle _____ there isn't any air in one of the tires.
   A. despite   B. because   C. although   D. but

2. I got to class on time _____ I had missed my bus.
   A. even though   B. nevertheless   C. because   D. despite

3. Brian used to be an active person, but now he has to limit his activities _____ problems with his health.
   A. nevertheless   B. because of   C. although   D. in spite of

4. It should be easy for Bob to find more time to spend with his children _____ he no longer has to work in the evenings and on weekends.
   A. even though   B. now that   C. due to   D. but

5. Jake is a very good student of languages. His brother Michael, _____, has never been able to master another language.
   A. therefore   B. even though
   C. whereas   D. on the other hand

6. The ancient Aztecs of Mexico had no technology for making tools from metal. _____, they had sharp knives and spears made from a stone called obsidian.
   A. Whereas   B. Although   C. Nevertheless   D. Despite

7. Roberta missed the meeting without a good reason _____ she had been told that it was critical that she be there. I wouldn't want to be in her shoes at work tomorrow.
   A. despite   B. despite the fact that   C. even   D. however

8. I usually enjoy attending amateur productions in small community theaters. The play we attended last night, _____, was so bad that I wanted to leave after the first act.
   A. therefore   B. however   C. whereas   D. even though

9. Some snakes are poisonous, _____ others are harmless.
   A. but   B. so   C. for   D. despite

10. Most 15th century Europeans believed that the world was flat and that a ship could conceivably sail off the end of the earth. _____, many sailors of the time refused to venture forth with explorers into unknown waters.
    A. Due to the fact that   B. Nevertheless   C. Therefore   D. Whereas

◇ **PRACTICE 10—GUIDED STUDY:** Cause/effect and opposition. (Charts 8-6 → 8-9 and 9-1 → 9-3)

Directions: Show the relationship between the ideas by adding any of the following expressions, as appropriate:

because	*because of*	*while/whereas*	*on the other hand*
since	*due to*	*nevertheless*	*in spite of*
now that	*even though*	*however*	*despite*
therefore	*although*		

1. It was still hot in the room ____**even though / although**____ I had turned on the air conditioner.

2. Several people in the crowd became ill and fainted ____**due to / because of**____ the extreme heat.

3. The gardener trimmed the branches on the cherry tree _____ I asked him not to.

4. The meat of the puffer fish can cause paralysis or even death if it is improperly prepared. _____, it remains a delicacy in Japan for brave diners.

5. _____ everyone disagreed with him, Brian went ahead with his original plan for the company.

6. The first mention of the game of chess appears in an Indian text written almost 1500 years ago. _____ its ancient beginnings, it remains one of the most widely played games in the world today.

7. Alice heard a siren and saw the flashing lights of a police car in her rear-view mirror. _____, she quickly pulled over to the side of the road and stopped.

8. Most adults carry around certain attitudes and prejudices about the world around them. Most children, _____, enter new situations without such preconceived notions.

9. They often have to close all of the ski areas in the mountains _____ severe weather conditions and avalanche danger.

10. _____ paper was first developed by the ancient Chinese, its English name comes from the word *papyrus*, the name of an Egyptian water plant.

11. The supervisor must know what everyone in the department is doing _____ all responsibility for error will fall on her shoulders.

12. _____ aspirin is relatively safe for most adults, it should be administered very carefully to children, if at all. It can be dangerous to children's health.

13. The peanut is used today to make everything from cosmetics to explosives _____ the pioneering scientific work of George Washington Carver in the 1910s and 1920s.

14. In ancient China, yellow was considered to be an imperial color. _____, only the emperor was allowed to wear it. No one else could have yellow clothing of any kind.

15. _____ the abacus had been in use in Asia since ancient times, many in the Western world credited 19-year-old Blaise Pascal, a Frenchman, with inventing the first calculating machine in 1642.

16. _____ she thought she heard the telephone ringing, Marge turned the TV down—only to discover it had been a telephone on the show she was watching.

◇ PRACTICE 11—GUIDED STUDY: *"If clauses."* (Chart 9-4)

Directions: Using the given possibilities, make sentences using *if*. Pay special attention to verb forms.

1. My car will probably not start tomorrow morning.
   → *If my car **doesn't start** tomorrow morning, **I'll take** the bus to work.*
2. Sometimes my car doesn't start in the morning.
   → *If my car **doesn't start** in the morning, **I take** the bus to work.*

3. Sometimes I have free time.
4. Maybe I will have some free time tomorrow.
5. I might not be able to come to the meeting this afternoon.
6. Sometimes I can't attend a meeting at my office.
7. You will probably be too tired to finish your work this afternoon.
8. Perhaps I won't be able to get a ticket for Flight 605 Tuesday morning.
9. We might not have enough money to take our trip next month.
10. People might continue to destroy their environment.

◇ PRACTICE 12—GUIDED STUDY: Using *whether or not* and *even if*. (Chart 9-5)

Directions: Complete the sentences with your own words.

Examples:
   Even if . . . , I'm not going to go.
   → *Even if I get an invitation to the reception, I'm not going to go.*

   . . . whether I feel better or not.
   → *I have to go to work tomorrow whether I feel better or not.*

1. . . . even if the weather improves.
2. Even if . . . , you may not pass the course.
3. Getting that job depends on whether or not . . . .
4. Even if I have a lot of work to do, ...
5. . . . whether you want me to or not.
6. I won't tell you even if . . . .
7. . . . even if it's past midnight.
8. Please tell me soon whether or not . . . so that I can decide what I'm going to do.

◇ PRACTICE 13—SELFSTUDY: Using *in case* and *in the event that*. (Chart 9-6)

Directions: Complete the sentences by using *in case*. Decide if it goes in the first blank or in the second blank. Add necessary punctuation and capitalization.

1. _____*In case*_____ you need to get in touch with me _____,_____ I'll be in my office until late this evening.

2. _____*W*_____ we'll be at the Swan Hotel _____*in case*_____ you need to call us.

3. _____ you'd better take your raincoat with you _____ the weather changes. It could rain before you get home again.

4. Mary is willing to work with you on your design project. _____ you find that you need help with it _____ she'll be back in town next Monday and can meet with you then.

5. _____ my boss has to stay near a phone all weekend _____ the company wants him to go to London to close the deal they've been working on all month.

6. _____ I'm not back in time to make dinner _____ I put the phone number for carry-out Chinese food on the refrigerator. You can call and order the food for yourself.

Complete the sentences using *in the event that*.

7. _____*In the event that*_____ Janet is late for work again tomorrow _____,_____ she will be fired.

8. Are you sure you're taking enough money with you? _____ you'd better take a credit card with you _____ you run out of cash.

9. The political situation is getting more unstable and dangerous. _____ my family plans to leave the country _____ there is a civil war.

10. Just to be on the safe side, _____ I always take a change of clothes in my carry-on bag _____ the airline loses my luggage.

11. The cheapest way to get from an airport to a hotel is to take an airport bus, but I'm not sure if River City has one. _____ there is no airport bus _____ you can always take a taxi.

12. Ann is one of five people nominated for an award to be given at the banquet this evening. _____ she has already prepared an acceptance speech _____ she wins it tonight.

◇ PRACTICE 14—SELFSTUDY: Using *unless* vs. *if* and *only if*. (Charts 9-7 and 9-8)

Directions: Choose the correct answer.

1. Most people you meet will be polite to you __*B*__ you are polite to them.
   A. unless   B. if

2. I can't buy a car _____ I save enough money.
   A. unless   B. only if

3. Eggs will not hatch _____ they are kept at the proper temperature.
   A. unless   B. only if

4. Our kids are allowed to watch television after dinner _____ they have finished their homework. Homework must come first.
   A. unless   B. only if

5. I'll give you a hand _____ you need it, but I hope I don't hurt my back.
   A. unless   B. if

6. I'm afraid the battery is dead. _____ I buy a new one, the car won't start.
   A. unless   B. if

7. My sister can fall asleep under any conditions, but I can't get to sleep _____ the light is off and the room is perfectly quiet.
   A. unless   B. if

8. There can be peace in the world _____ all nations sincerely lend their energy to that effort.
   A. unless   B. only if

9. Alice will tutor you in math _____ you promise to do everything she says.
   A. unless   B. only if

10. Oscar won't pass his math course _____ he gets a tutor.
    A. unless   B. only if

11. I won't be involved in this project _____ you assure me that we won't be violating any laws.
    A. unless   B. if

12. I'll prepare a really special dinner _____ you all promise to be home on time this evening. Let's plan on an old-fashioned sit-down dinner with the whole family at the table at once.
    A. unless   B. only if

◇ **PRACTICE 15—SELFSTUDY: Using *if, only if, unless,* and *provided/providing that.* (Charts 9-7 and 9-8)**

Directions: Choose the correct words in italics so that the sentences make sense.

1. I'm   *going to go,* (*not going to go*)   to the park unless the weather is nice.

2. I'm going to go to the park unless it   *rains, doesn't rain.*

3. I'll pass the course provided that I   *pass, don't pass*   the final examination.

4. Tom doesn't like to work. He'll get a job   *unless, only if*   he has to.

5. I   *always eat, never eat*   breakfast unless I get up late and don't have enough time.

6. I always finish my homework   *even if, only if*   I'm sleepy and want to go to bed.

7. Grass grows provided that it   *gets, doesn't get*   enough water.

8. You   *will, won't*   learn to play the violin well unless you practice every day.

9. Even if the president calls,   *wake, don't wake*   me up. I don't want to talk to anyone. I want to sleep.

10. Jack is going to come to the game with us today   *if, unless*   his boss gives him the afternoon off.

11. *Borrow, Don't borrow*   money from your friends unless you absolutely must.

12. I'll get tickets to the concert provided that there   *are still some, aren't any*   available.

◇ PRACTICE 16—SELFSTUDY: Using *only if* vs. *if*: subject-verb inversion. (Chart 9-8)

Directions: Change the position of the adverb clause to the front of the sentence. Make any necessary changes in the verb of the main clause.

1. I can finish this work on time only if you help me.
   → **Only if** you help me **can I finish** *this work on time.*

2. I can finish this work on time if you help me.
   → **If** you help me, **I can finish** *this work on time.*

3. I will go only if I am invited.

4. I will go if I am invited.

5. I eat only if I am hungry.

6. I usually eat some fruit if I am hungry during the morning.

7. You will be considered for that job only if you know both Arabic and Spanish.

8. John goes to the market only if the refrigerator is empty.

9. I will tell you the truth about what happened only if you promise not to get angry.

10. I won't discuss it any further if you get angry.

◇ PRACTICE 17—GUIDED STUDY: Expressing conditions. (Charts 9-5 → 9-8)

Directions: Complete the sentences using your own words.

Examples:
. . . only if you can prove to me that your assumptions are correct about next year's potential profits.
   → *I will support your position with the boss only if you can prove to me that your assumptions are correct about next year's potential profits.*

There's a 10 percent discount on everything today provided that . . . .
   → *There's a 10 percent discount on everything today provided that* **you have one of the coupons from today's newspaper.**

1. I'm never late to class unless . . . .
2. . . . only if I ask her to.
3. High school students shouldn't quit school even if . . . .
4. . . . providing that my flight leaves on time.
5. . . . unless the doctor says I shouldn't.
6. Mr. Crane will take the temporary assignment out of town only if . . . .
7. My neighbor will take care of my apartment while I'm out of town provided that . . . .
8. The price of oil will remain stable if . . . .
9. . . . only if you explain your reasons completely.
10. Providing that all of our work is finished, ...
11. I'm going to be gone for three days unless . . . .
12. I will interview for that job provided that . . . .

◇ PRACTICE 18—SELFSTUDY: Using *otherwise*. (Chart 9-9)

Directions: Make two sentences. Show the relationship between them by using *otherwise*. In the first sentence, use a modal auxiliary or similar expression: *should, had better, have to, must.*

1. If you don't eat less and get more exercise, you won't lose weight.
   → *You should (had better/have to/must) eat less and get more exercise. Otherwise, you won't lose weight.*

2. The children can watch TV tonight only if they finish all of their chores.
   → *The children have to (had better/should/must) finish all of their chores. Otherwise, they cannot watch TV tonight.*

3. Unless you speak up now, the boss will go ahead without knowing that you don't agree.

4. If you don't stop at the store on your way home from work, we won't have anything to eat for dinner tonight.

5. Unless you think it through very carefully, you won't come up with the right answer.

6. If we don't catch any fish this morning, we're going to have beans for dinner again.

7. It's going to be very difficult to finish on time if you don't get someone in to help you.

8. Maria is probably going to lose her job unless she finds a way to convince the boss that the error was unavoidable.

◇ PRACTICE 19—SELFSTUDY: Expressing conditions. (Charts 9-5 → 9-8)

Directions: Complete the sentences with any appropriate form of the verb "pass."

1. Keith will graduate if he _____*passes*_____ all of his courses.

2. Sam won't graduate if he ____*doesn't pass*____ all of his courses.

3. Ed won't graduate unless he _____ all of his courses.

4. Sue will graduate only if she _____ all of her courses.

5. Jessica will graduate even if she _____ all of her courses.

6. Alex won't graduate even if he _____ all of his courses.

7. Jennifer will graduate provided that she _____ all of her courses.

8. Amy won't graduate in the event that she _____ all of her courses.

9. Jerry _____ all of his courses. Otherwise, he won't graduate.

10. Carolyn _____ all of her courses, or else she won't graduate.

◇ PRACTICE 20—GUIDED STUDY: Summary of relationship words. (Charts 8-5 and 9-10)

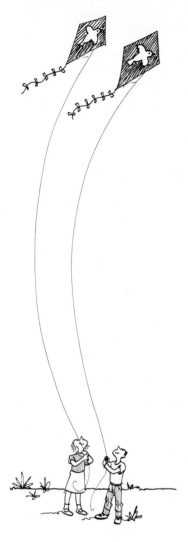

Directions: Pair up with another student.
STUDENT A: Speak the given words and add your own words (but without completing the sentence). You should say approximately half of the sentence.
STUDENT B: Complete Student A's sentence.

Example: Although I . . . .
STUDENT A: *Although I wanted to go to the park and fly a kite,* . . .
STUDENT B: *Although I wanted to go to the park and fly a kite,* **I went to my English class because I really need to improve my English.**

1. Even if I . . . .
2. Because I . . . .
3. By the time I . . . .
4. Even though I . . . .
5. The next time I . . . .
6. Despite the fact that I . . . .
7. Every time I . . . .
8. In the event that you . . . .
9. Unless I . . . .
10. Since I . . . .
11. Only if I . . . .
12. Now that I . . . .
13. While some people are . . . .
14. While I was walking . . . .

◇ PRACTICE 21—SELFSTUDY: Summary of relationship words. (Chart 9-10)

Directions: Choose the best completion.

1. The sky was gray and cloudy. _____, we went to the beach.
   A. Consequently   B. Nevertheless   C. Even though   D. In spite of

2. I turned on the fan _____ the room was hot.
   A. due to   B. despite   C. even though   D. because

3. Sam and I will meet you at the restaurant tonight _____ we can find a babysitter.
   A. although   B. unless   C. otherwise   D. only if

4. Carol showed up for the meeting _____ I asked her not to be there.
   A. even though   B. despite   C. provided that   D. because

5. You must lend me the money for the trip. _____, I won't be able to go.
   A. Consequently   B. Nevertheless   C. Otherwise   D. Although

6. The road will remain safe _____ the flood washes out the bridge.
   A. as long as   B. unless   C. providing that   D. since

7. The roles of men and women were not the same in ancient Greece. For example, men were both participants and spectators in the ancient Olympics. Women, _____, were forbidden to attend or participate.
    A. nevertheless   B. on the other hand   C. therefore   D. otherwise

8. The windows were all left open. _____, the room was a real mess after the windstorm.
    A. Nevertheless   B. However   C. Consequently   D. Otherwise

9. _____ I can't make the presentation myself, I've asked my assistant to be prepared to do it for me.
    A. For   B. In the event that   C. Only if   D. On the other hand

10. It looks like they're going to succeed _____ their present difficulties.
    A. despite   B. because of   C. even though   D. yet

11. _____ Marge is an honest person, I still wonder whether she's telling the truth about the incident.
    A. In spite of   B. Since   C. Though   D. In the event that

12. The professor told me that I was doing well, _____ my final grade was awful!
    A. so   B. therefore   C. in spite of   D. yet

13. _____ Beth has a new car, she no longer takes the commuter train to work. She drives to work every day.
    A. Now that   B. While   C. Although   D. In case

14. You'd better give me your answer quickly, _____ I'll withdraw the invitation.
    A. although   B. nevertheless   C. even though   D. or else

15. I have to go to the meeting _____ I want to or not.
    A. provided that   B. whether   C. even if   D. only if

16. What time do you expect Ted to be home? I must talk to him. I usually go to bed around ten, but tell him to call me tonight _____ it's past midnight.
    A. however   B. in case   C. even if   D. as long as

17. _____ you're going to the fruit market, would you please pick up a few apples for me?
    A. Even if   B. Although   C. So   D. As long as

18. I guess I'm a soft touch. I just lent Jan some money for lunch _____ she never paid me back my last loan.
    A. even though   B. unless   C. or else   D. only if

19. I think I did okay in my speech last night _____ I'd had almost no sleep for 24 hours.
    A. even   B. in spite of   C. unless   D. despite the fact that

20. I asked Angela to run the office while I'm gone _____ I know I can depend on her.
    A. unless   B. since   C. although   D. therefore

21. _____ the secret of how to make silk remained inside Asia, Europeans were forced to pay incredibly high sums of money for this mysterious material to be brought overland to Europe.
    A. Although   B. Only if   C. Due to   D. As long as

22. Ancient Egyptians mummified their dead through the use of chemicals, _____ ancient Peruvians mumified their dead through natural processes by putting dead bodies in extremely dry desert caves.
    A. whereas   B. because   C. even though   D. whether or not

◇ **PRACTICE 22—GUIDED STUDY:** Summary of relationship words. (Chart 9-10)

Directions: Form a group of 4 to 6 people. One of you should begin a "chain sentence" by speaking the given words plus one, two, or three additional words. Each of the others should add one, two, or three words until the sentence is completed. The maximum number of words a person can add is *three*. When you complete your sentence, one person in the group should write it down (with correct punctuation, spelling, and capitalization).

Example: Although education is . . . .
STUDENT A : Although education is **important**, ...
STUDENT B : Although education is important, **some students** . . . .
STUDENT C : Although education is important, some students **would rather** . . . .
STUDENT D : Although education is important, some students would rather **fly a kite** . . . .
STUDENT A : Although education is important, some students would rather fly a kite **than** . . . .
STUDENT B : Although education is important, some students would rather fly a kite than **go to class**.
FINAL SENTENCE: → *Although education is important, some students would rather fly a kite than go to class.*

1. Because we are . . . .
2. Even though students don't . . . .
3. Unless students . . . .
4. In the event that an earthquake occurs in . . . .
5. Students have to study. Otherwise . . . .
6. In spite of the fact that students . . . .
7. Even if we . . . .
8. Only if . . . .
9. Being a student can be stressful. Therefore, ...
10. I was so confused when the teacher . . . .
11. Despite . . . .
12. Now that we . . . .

◇ **PRACTICE 23—GUIDED STUDY:** Summary of relationship words. (Chart 9-10)

Directions: Complete the sentences with your own words. Add necessary punctuation and capitalization.

Example:
Mary has to wear glasses otherwise _____
→ *Mary has to wear glasses.* ***Otherwise, she can't see words clearly when she reads.***

1. _____ but I washed it anyway.

2. Only if _____ will I lend you the money for a red motorcycle.

3. I _____ only because I thought that everyone had already finished eating.

4. _____ although she had had a temperature and chills all night.

5. Next Monday is a national holiday therefore _____

6. _____ in the event that my suit isn't back from the cleaners.

7. As long as you have some extra money this month _____

8. I brought my brother with me just in case _____

9. Parents need to be involved in their children's education however _____

10. Inasmuch as _____ is my favorite color _____

11. I was so sure I was right that _____

12. The banana was brown and mushy nevertheless _____

13. _____ often have to work at odd hours of the day or night on the

other hand _____ usually work daytime hours only.

14. Since I'm going to be out of town for the next two weeks _____

15. Since I came here _____

16. Most wild animals will attack a human being only if _____

17. There was a major accident on the interstate highway consequently _____

18. I wanted to relax so _____

19. The population of the city has increased so rapidly _____

20. I am getting an education so that _____

◇ **PRACTICE 24—GUIDED STUDY: Punctuation. (Chapters 6 → 9)**

Directions: Add appropriate punctuation and capitalization to clarify the following passages.

1. I did not expect to get a pay raise nevertheless I accepted when my boss offered it.

→ *I did not expect to get a pay raise. Nevertheless, I accepted when my boss offered it.*

2. Although a computer has tremendous power and speed it cannot think for itself a human operator is needed to give a computer instructions for it cannot initially tell itself what to do.

3. Being a lawyer in private practice I work hard but I do not go to my office on either Saturday or Sunday if clients insist upon seeing me on the weekend they have to come to my home.

4. Whenever my father goes fishing we know we will have fish to eat for dinner for even if he doesn't catch any he stops at the fish market on his way home and buys some.

5. The goatherd who supposedly discovered coffee is a legendary rather than historical figure no one knows for sure that the first coffee was discovered when an Ethiopian goatherd noticed that his goats did not fall asleep all night long after they had eaten the leaves and berries of coffee plants.

6. Whenever the weather is nice I walk to school but when it is cold or wet I either take the bus or get a ride with one of my friends even though my brother has a car I never ask him to take me to school because he is very busy he has a new job and has recently gotten married so he doesn't have time to drive me to and from school anymore I know he would give me a ride if I asked him to however I don't want to bother him.

7. The common cold which is the most widespread of all diseases continues to plague humanity despite the efforts of scientists to find its prevention and cure even though colds are minor illnesses they are one of the principal causes of absence from school and work people of all ages get colds but children and adults who live with children get the most colds can be dangerous for elderly people because they can lead to other infections I have had three colds so far this year I eat the right kinds of food get enough rest and exercise regularly nevertheless I still get at least one cold a year.

◇ PRACTICE 25—GUIDED STUDY: Showing relationships. (Chapters 8 and 9)

Directions: Using the words in parentheses, combine the following sentences to show the relationships between the ideas. Punctuate and capitalize correctly.

Example:
   a. Jack hates going to the dentist.
   b. He should see his dentist soon.
   c. He has a very bad toothache.
      (RELATIONSHIP WORDS TO USE: *even though, because*)
   → *Even though Jack hates going to the dentist, he should see his dentist soon because he has a very bad toothache.*

1. a. You may really mean what you say.
   b. I'll give you one more chance.
   c. You have to give me your best effort.
   d. You'll lose your job.
      (RELATIONSHIP WORDS: *if, but, otherwise*)

2. a. The weather is bad.
   b. I'm going to stay home.
   c. The weather may change.
   d. I don't want to go to the picnic.
      (RELATIONSHIP WORDS: *due to, even if*)

3. a. The children had eaten lunch.
   b. They got hungry in the middle of the afternoon.
   c. I took them to the market.
   d. They wanted to get some fruit for a snack.
   e. We went home for dinner.
      (RELATIONSHIP WORDS: *even though, therefore, so that, before*)

4. a. Robert is totally exhausted after playing tennis.
   b. Marge isn't even tired.
   c. She ran around a lot more during the game.
      (RELATIONSHIP WORDS: *whereas, in spite of the fact that*)

5. a. My boss promised me that I could have two full weeks.
   b. It seems that I can't take my vacation after all.
   c. I have to train the new personnel this summer.
   d. I may not get a vacation in the fall either.
   e. I will be angry.
      (RELATIONSHIP WORDS: *even though, because, if*)

6. a. Paul might finish his deliveries early this evening.
   b. He'll join us in time for dinner.
   c. You should make a reservation for him.
   d. The restaurant may not be able to accommodate all of us at the last minute.
      (RELATIONSHIP WORDS: *in the event that, therefore, otherwise*)

7. a. Education, business, and government are all becoming more dependent on computers.
   b. It is advisable for all students to have basic computer skills.
   c. They graduate from high school and enter the work force or college.
   d. A course called "Computer Literacy" has recently become a requirement for graduation from Westside High School.
   e. Maybe you will want more information about this course.
   f. You can call the academic counselor at the high school.
      (RELATIONSHIP WORDS: *inasmuch as, before, therefore, if*)

8. a. Many animals are most vulnerable to predators when they are grazing.
   b. Giraffes are most vulnerable when they are drinking.
   c. They must spread their legs awkwardly to lower their long necks to the water in front of them.
   d. It is difficult and time-consuming for them to stand up straight again to escape a predator.
   e. Once they are up and running, they are faster than most of their predators.
      (RELATIONSHIP WORDS: *while, consequently, however*)

◇ **PRACTICE 26—GUIDED STUDY:** Showing relationships. (Chapters 6 → 9)

Directions: Write out the sentences, completing them with your own words. (Warning: Some of your sentences will have to get a little complicated.) Some punctuation is given; add other punctuation as necessary.

Example:

I have trouble _____, so I _____ when I _____
→ *I have trouble* **remembering people's names,** *so I* **have to concentrate** *when I* **first meet someone.**

I wanted to _____. Nevertheless, I _____ because _____
→ *I wanted to* **go to Chicago.** *Nevertheless,* **I stayed home** *because* **I had to study for final exams.**

1. _____ sore throat. Nevertheless, _____.

2. I _____. My _____, on the other hand, _____.

3. When a small, black insect _____, I _____ because _____.

4. I _____ because _____. However, _____.

5. Even though I told _____ that _____, _____.

6. According to the newspaper, now that _____. Therefore, _____.

7. Since neither the man who _____ nor _____, I _____.

8. _____, but in the event that _____, _____.

9. When people who _____, _____ because _____.

10. Since I didn't know whose _____, I _____.

11. Even though the book which _____, I _____.

12. What did the woman who _____ when you _____?

◇ **PRACTICE 27—GUIDED STUDY:** Giving examples. (Chart 9-11)

Directions: Add examples to the given sentences.

1. Countries such as _____ have large uninhabited areas. Other countries, such as _____, are densely populated.

2. Animals such as _____ make good house pets, but others such as _____ do not.

3. Colors that are bright and gaudy, such as _____, are best to wear when you want to stand out in a crowd. If you want to keep a low profile, however, colors such as _____ are more appropriate.

4. Hard metals and alloys such as _____ are used to produce exceptionally strong objects, while softer metals such as _____ are often shaped into jewelry or works of art.

5. Some things that we read, such as _____, engage our minds and make us think. Other things we read, however, such as _____, are strictly for entertainment.

6. There are many ways in which Paul could improve his health. For example, _____
_____.

7. Some television programs are educational, for example, _____.

8. We could get a fun gift for Anna on her birthday, something that would really surprise and delight her. For example, _____. Being a student, however, Anna would probably prefer something useful, such as _____.

9. An adjective (e.g., _____) usually describes a noun, but an adverb (e.g., _____) usually describes the action of a verb.

10. Some English words have the same pronunciation but different spelling, e.g., _____
_____.

◇ **PRACTICE 28—SELFSTUDY: Continuing the same idea. (Chart 9-12)**

Directions: Add *moreover/in addition/furthermore* where appropriate.

1. Government money is essential to successful research at our university. For example, much of the research in the medical school is funded by government grants. Such departments as physics, chemistry, computer science, and engineering now rely increasingly on government funding.
   → *Government money is essential to successful research at our university. For example, much of the research in the medical school is funded by government grants.* **Moreover/In addition/Furthermore,** *such departments as physics, chemistry, computer science, and engineering now rely increasingly on government funding.*

2. Applicants for the position must fulfill certain requirements. They need a college degree and two years' experience in the field. They must have computer skills. Two letters of recommendation should be submitted along with the application.

3. There are several reasons why I write in my diary every day. Writing a diary allows me to reflect on a day's events and their meanings. As the Greek philosopher Plato said, ''A life that is unexamined is not worth living.'' I like the idea of keeping a record of my life to share with my children at a later date. Writing in a diary is calming. It forces me to take time out of my busy day to rest and think quiet thoughts.

4. If you are interested in the arts, you should come to visit my city, Montreal. Montreal is a leading cultural center in North America. You can go to the Museum of Fine Arts to see displays of works by Canadian artists, past and present. Montreal has a world-famous symphony orchestra. It has numerous theaters. One of them, the International Theater, performs plays in several languages.

◇ PRACTICE 29—GUIDED STUDY: Error analysis. (Chapters 1 → 9)

Directions: The following passages are taken from student writing. Pretend you are the editor for these students. Rewrite the passages. Correct any errors and make whatever revisions in phrasing or vocabulary you feel will help the writers say what they intended to say.

Example:

My idea of the most important thing in life. It is to be healthy. Because a person can't enjoy life without health.

→ *In my opinion, the most important thing in life is good health, for a person cannot enjoy life fully without it.*

1. We went shopping after ate dinner. But the stores were closed. We had to go back home even we hadn't found what were we looking for.

2. I want explain that I know alot of grammars but is my problem I haven't enough vocabularies.

3. When I got lost in the bus station a kind man helped me, he explained how to read the huge bus schedule on the wall. Took me to the window to buy a ticket and showed me where was my bus, I will always appreciate his kindness.

4. I had never understand the important of know English language. Until I worked at a large international company.

5. Since I was young my father found an American woman to teach me and my brothers English, but when we move to other town my father wasn't able to find other teacher for other five years.

6. I was surprised to see the room that I was given at the dormitory. Because there aren't any furniture, and dirty.

7. When I met Mr. Lee for the first time, we played ping pong at the student center even though we can't communicate very well, but we had a good time.

8. Because the United States is a large and also big country. It means that there're various kinds of people live there and it has a diverse population.

9. My grammar class was start at 10:35. When the teacher was coming to class, she returned the last quiz to my classmates and I. After we have had another quiz.

10. The first time I went skiing. I was afraid to go down the hill. But somewhere from a little corner of my head kept shouting, "why not! Give it a try. You'll make it!" After stand around a couple of more minutes with my index finger in my mouth. Finally, I decided to go down that hill.

11. If a wife has a work, her husband should share the houseworks with her. If both of them help, the houseworks can be finish much faster.

12. This is a story about a man who had a big garden. One day he was sleeping in his garden. Then he woke up and he ate some fruit. Then he picked some apples and he walked to a small river and he saw a beautiful woman was on the other side. And he gave her some apples and then she gave him a loaf of bread. The two of them walked back to the garden. Then some children came and were playing games with him. Everyone was laughing and smiling. Then

one child destroyed a flower and the man became angry and he said to them, "Get out of here." Then the children left and the beautiful woman left. Then the man built a wall around his garden and would not let anyone in. He stayed in his garden all alone for the rest of his life.

◇ **PRACTICE TEST A—SELFSTUDY: Showing relationships between ideas. (Chapter 9)**

Directions: Choose the best completion.

Example:

   _C_ *I heard the telephone ring, I didn't answer it.*
   A. Because   B. Only if   C. Even though   D. Provided that

1. _____ the salary meets my expectations, I will accept the job offer.
   A. Due to   B. Even if   C. Provided that   D. Unless

2. To power their inventions, people have made use of natural energy sources, _____ coal, oil, water, and steam.
   A. in addition to   B. as   C. and they use   D. such as

3. _____ excellent art museums, Moscow has a world-famous ballet company.
   A. Because of   B. In spite of   C. In case of   D. In addition to

4. It is still a good idea to know how to type. _____ the many technological advances in typewriters and word processors, a skilled operator remains indispensable.
   A. Because of   B. In spite of   C. In case of   D. In addition to

5. Even though a duck may live on water, it stays dry _____ the oil on its feathers. The oil prevents the water from soaking through the feathers and reaching its skin.
   A. due to   B. besides   C. in spite of   D. in the event of

6. Alex cannot express himself clearly and correctly in writing. He will never advance in his job _____ he improves his language skills.
   A. otherwise   B. if   C. only if   D. unless

7. _____ there was no electricity, I was able to read because I had a candle.
   A. Unless   B. Even though   C. Even   D. Only if

8. A fire must have a readily available supply of oxygen. _____, it will stop burning.
   A. Consequently   B. Furthermore   C. Otherwise   D. However

9. I studied Spanish for four years in high school. _____, I had trouble talking with people when I was traveling in Spain.
   A. Therefore   B. On the other hand   C. Moreover   D. Nevertheless

10. I'm sorry you've decided not to go with us on the river trip, but _____ you change your mind, there will still be enough room on the boat for you.
   A. even   B. nevertheless   C. in the event that   D. provided that

11. I like to keep the windows open at night no matter how cold it gets. My wife, _____, prefers a warm bedroom with all windows tightly shut.
   A. nevertheless   B. consequently   C. on the other hand   D. moreover

12. Some fish can survive only in salt water, _____ other species can live only in fresh water.
   A. whereas   B. unless   C. if   D. since

13. _____ Jason became famous, he has ignored his old friends. He shouldn't do that.
   A. If   B. Ever since   C. Even though   D. Due to

14. We're going to lose this game _____ the team doesn't start playing better soon.
   A. if   B. unless   C. although   D. whereas

15. My two children are cooking dinner for the family for the first time tonight. _____ the food is terrible, I'm going to enjoy this meal very much. It will be fun to have them cook for me for a change.
    A. Only if   B. If   C. Even if   D. Provided that

16. Jack insisted that he didn't need any help, _____ I helped him anyway.
    A. and   B. so   C. besides   D. but

17. Florida is famous for its tourist attractions. Its coastline offers excellent white sand beaches. _____, it has warm, sunny weather.
    A. Otherwise   B. Furthermore   C. Nevertheless   D. On the other hand

18. The flowers will soon start to bloom _____ winter is gone and the weather is beginning to get warmer.
    A. even if   B. now that   C. so   D. even though

19. Only if you promise to study hard _____ to tutor you.
    A. will I agree   B. agree I   C. I agree   D. I will agree

20. Camels have either one hump or two humps. The Arabian camel has one hump. The Bactrian camel, _____, has two humps.
    A. nevertheless   B. however   C. furthermore   D. otherwise

◇ PRACTICE TEST B—GUIDED STUDY: Showing relationships between ideas. (Chapter 9)

Directions: Choose the best completion.

Example:
    __C__ *I heard the telephone ring, I didn't answer it.*
    A. *Because*   B. *Only if*   C. *Even though*   D. *Provided that*

1. Mr. Jackson hopes to avoid surgery. He will not agree to the operation _____ he is convinced that it is absolutely necessary.
    A. in the event that B. unless   C. if   D. only if

2. Some English words have the same pronunciation _____ they are spelled differently, for example, *dear* and *deer*.
    A. unless   B. even though   C. since   D. only if

3. Olives are a principal source of cooking oil, but by no means the only source. _____ olives, cooking oil can be extracted from coconuts, corn, and sunflower seeds.
    A. Because of   B. In spite of   C. In case of   D. In addition to

4. I couldn't use the pay phone, _____ I didn't have any coins with me.
    A. yet   B. despite   C. for   D. even though

5. I have to eat beakfast in the morning. _____, I get grouchy and hungry before my lunch break.
    A. Consequently   B. Furthermore   C. Otherwise   D. However

6. I need to find an apartment before I can move. _____ I can find one in the next week or so, I will move to Chicago the first of next month.
    A. Provided that   B. Even if   C. Due to   D. Only if

7. Tom is trying to reduce the amount of fat he eats. Red meat is high in fat. Tom eats a lot of fish but avoids red meat _____ its high fat content.
    A. in the event of B. besides   C. in spite of   D. because of

8. _____ want to take a train trip across western Canada, but my traveling companion wants to fly to Mexico City for our vacation.
    A. Although I   B. Even if I   C. I   D. Nevertheless I

9. Ms. Moore, the school counselor, has had years of experience dealing with student problems. _____, she is sometimes confronted by a problem that she cannot handle by herself.
   A. Therefore   B. Nevertheless   C. Otherwise   D. On the other hand

10. Right now all the seats on that flight are taken, sir. _____ there is a cancellation, I will call you.
    A. In the event that   B. Nevertheless   C. But   D. Even if

11. A newborn baby can neither walk nor crawl. A newborn antelope, _____, can run within minutes of birth.
    A. however   B. nevertheless   C. otherwise   D. even though

12. You must obey the speed limits on public roads. They are designed to keep you safe. You shouldn't exceed the speed limit _____ you are an experienced race car driver.
    A. only if   B. even if   C. if   D. provided that

13. My nose got sunburned _____ I wore a hat with a wide brim to shade my face.
    A. if   B. since   C. because   D. even though

14. Do you like jazz? You should go to the jazz festival _____ you like that kind of music.
    A. if   B. unless   C. although   D. while

15. Peter works hard at everything he does. His brother, _____, seldom puts out much effort.
    A. on the other hand   B. otherwise   C. furthermore   D. consequently

16. I don't understand why, but my neighbor Mr. Morrow doesn't seem to like me. He never smiles at me or speaks to me _____ the many efforts I have made to be friendly and neighborly.
    A. because of   B. in spite of   C. in case of   D. in addition to

17. The festival has many attractions. It will include contemporary orchestral music and an opera. _____, there will be poetry readings and theatrical presentations.
    A. Otherwise   B. Furthermore   C. Nevertheless   D. On the other hand

18. The bread was old and stale, _____ Martha ate it anyway.
    A. and   B. so   C. besides   D. but

19. Minerals _____ nickel, copper, and zinc can be found in sea water.
    A. as examples   B. such as   C. in an example   D. as

20. Only if you get to the theater early _____ a chance to get a ticket for tonight's performance.
    A. you will have   B. have   C. you have   D. will you have

CHAPTER 10
Conditional Sentences

◇ **PRACTICE 1—SELFSTUDY:** Conditional sentences. (Charts 10-1 → 10-4)

Directions: Answer the questions about each conditional sentence with "yes" or "no".

1. *If the weather had been good yesterday, our picnic would not have been canceled.*
   a. Was the picnic canceled? ___**yes**___
   b. Was the weather good? ___**no**___

2. *If I had an envelope and a stamp, I would mail this letter right now.*
   a. Do I have an envelope and a stamp right now? _____
   b. Do I want to mail this letter right now? _____
   c. Am I going to mail this letter right now? _____

3. *Ann would have made it to class on time this morning if the bus hadn't been late.*
   a. Did Ann try to make it to class on time? _____
   b. Did Ann make it to class on time? _____
   c. Was the bus late? _____

4. *If I were a carpenter, I would build my own house.*
   a. Do I want to build my own house? _____
   b. Am I going to build my own house? _____
   c. Am I a carpenter? _____

5. *If the hotel had been built to withstand an earthquake, it would not have collapsed.*
   a. Was the hotel built to withstand an earthquake? _____
   b. Did the hotel collapse? _____

6. *If I didn't have any friends, I would be lonely.*
   a. Am I lonely? _____
   b. Do I have friends? _____

7. *If Bob had asked me to keep the news a secret, I wouldn't have told anybody.*
   a. Did I tell anybody the news? _____
   b. Did Bob ask me to keep it a secret? _____

8. *If Thomas had sold his car, he would have to take the subway to work every morning.*
   a. Does Thomas have a car? _____
   b. Does he take the subway to work? _____

9. *If Ann and Jan, who are twins, dressed alike and had the same hairstyles, I wouldn't be able to tell them apart.*

    a. Do Ann and Jan dress alike? _____

    b. Do they have the same hairstyles? _____

    c. Can I tell them apart? _____

◇ **PRACTICE 2—SELFSTUDY:** Conditional sentences, present/future. (Charts 10-2 and 10-3)

Directions: Complete the sentences with the correct form of the verbs in parentheses. Some of the sentences are "contrary to fact" and some are not.

1. I am not an astronaut. If I (*be*) _____ **were** _____ an astronaut, I (*take*) _____ **would**
_____ **take** _____ my camera with me on the rocket ship next month.

2. Most people know that oil floats on water. If you pour oil on water, it (*float*)_____ **floats/**
_____ **will float** _____ .

3. If there (*be*) _____ no oxygen on earth, life as we know it (*exist, not*)
_____ .

4. My evening newspaper has been late every day this week. If the paper (*arrive, not*)
_____ on time today, I'm going to cancel my subscription.

5. If I (*be*) _____ a bird, I (*want, not*) _____ to live in a
cage.

6. Sea water is salty. If the oceans (*consist*) _____ of fresh water, there (*be*)
_____ plenty of water to irrigate all of the deserts in the world to provide
an abundant food supply for the entire population of the earth.

7. It is expensive to call across the ocean. However, if transoceanic telephone calls (*be*)
_____ cheap, I (*call*) _____ my family every day
and (*talk*) _____ for hours.

8. Tom's hobby is collecting stamps from all over the world. If he (*travel*) _____
to a new country, he (*spend, always*) _____ time looking for new stamps.
That's how he has acquired such a large collection of valuable stamps.

9. How old (*live, human beings*) _____ to be if all diseases in the world
(*be*) _____ completely eradicated?

10. If you boil water, it (*disappear*) _____ into the atmosphere as vapor.

11. If people (*have*) _____ paws instead of hands with fingers, the machines
we use in every day life (*have to*) _____ be constructed very differently.
We (*be, not*) _____ able to turn knobs, push small buttons, or hold tools
or utensils securely.

◇ **PRACTICE 3—SELFSTUDY: Conditional sentences, past time. (Chart 10-4)**

Directions: Complete the sentences with the words in parentheses. All of the sentences to complete are "contrary to fact."

1. I'm sorry you had to take a cab to the airport. I didn't know you needed a ride. If you (*tell*) ____*had told*____ me, I (*give*) ____*would have given*____ you a ride gladly.

2. You made a lot of unnecessary mistakes in your composition. If you (*use*) _____ a dictionary to check your spelling, you (*receive*) _____ a better grade.

3. A: Shh! Your father is taking a nap. Oh-oh. You woke him up.

   B: Gee, I'm sorry, Mom. If I (*realize*) _____ he was sleeping, I (*make, not*) _____ so much noise when I came in. But how was I supposed to know?

4. Many people were not satisfied with the leader after he took office. If they (*know*) _____ more about his planned economic programs, they (*vote, not*) _____ for him.

5. Last night Alex ruined his sweater when he washed it. If he (*read*) _____ the label, he (*wash, not*) _____ it in hot water.

6. A: Ever since I broke my foot, I haven't been able to get down to the basement to wash my clothes.

   B: Why didn't you say something? I (*come*) _____ over and (*wash*) _____ them for you if you (*ask*) _____ me.

   A: I know you (*come*) _____ right away if I (*call*) _____ you. I guess I just didn't want to bother you.

   B: Nonsense! What are good neighbors for?

7. A: Oh, no! I've lost it!

   B: Lost what?

   A: The address for my job interview this afternoon. I wrote it on a match book.

   B: A match book! If you (*write*) _____ the address in your appointment

   book where it belongs, you (*lose, not*) _____ it. When are you going to

   get organized?

8. A: Ann, (*you, take*) _____ that job if you (*know*) _____

   that you had to work nights?

   B: No way. I had no idea I'd have to work the late night hours they've had me working.

◇ **PRACTICE 4—SELFSTUDY: Conditional sentences. (Charts 10-1 → 10-4)**

   Directions: Complete the sentences with the words in parentheses.

   1. If I (*have*) _____ wings, I (*have to, not*) _____ take

   an airplane to fly home.

   2. This letter has got to be in Chicago in two days. I'm sure if I (*send*) _____

   it today, it will arrive in time.

   3. Hundreds of people became ill from eating contaminated meat during the last two weeks. If

   the government had responded more quickly to the crisis, fewer people (*suffer*) _____

   _____ food poisoning.

   4. (*People, be*) _____ able to fly if they (*have*) _____

   feathers instead of hair?

   5. What (*we, use*) _____ to look at ourselves when we comb our hair in the

   morning if we (*have, not*) _____ mirrors?

   6. A: I don't understand anything in this class. It's boring. And I'm getting a failing grade.
      B: If I (*feel*) _____ the way you do about it, I (*drop*) _____

   _____ the class as soon as possible.

   7. It's been a long drought. It hasn't rained for over a month. If it (*rain, not*) _____

   _____ soon, a lot of crops (*die*) _____. If the crops

   (*die*) _____, many people (*go*) _____ hungry this

   coming winter.

   8. I didn't know the Newtons were going to bring two other people to dinner last night. If

   anyone else (*bring*) _____ extra guests, we (*have, not*) _____

   _____ enough seats at the table.

   9. If television (*invent*) _____ in the eighteenth century, George Washington

   (*interview*) _____ regularly on the evening news.

10. A: I'm exhausted, and we're no closer to a solution to this problem after nine hours of work.

B: Why don't you go home and get some sleep, and I'll keep working. If I (*discover*)

_____ a solution before morning, I (*call*) _____

you immediately. I promise.

11. A: I can't believe that you haven't finished that report. What will I use in the committee

meeting at noon today?

B: I'm really sorry. If I (*know*) _____ you needed it today, I (*stay up*)

_____ all night last night and (*finish*) _____ it.

12. According to one scientific theory, an asteroid collided with the earth millions of years ago,

causing great changes in the earth's climate. Some scientists believe that if this asteroid

(*collide, not*) _____ with the earth, the dinosaurs (*become, not*) _____

_____ extinct. Can you imagine what the world (*be*) _____

like today if dinosaurs (*exist, still*) _____? Do you think it (*be*) _____

possible for dinosaurs and human beings to coexist on the same planet?

◇ PRACTICE 5—SELFSTUDY: Conditional sentences. (Charts 10-1 → 10-4)

Directions: Use the given information to make conditional sentences. Use *if*.

1. I was sick yesterday, so I didn't go to class.
   → *If I hadn't been sick yesterday, I would have gone to class.*
2. Because Alan never eats breakfast, he always overeats at lunch.
   → *If Alan ate breakfast, he wouldn't overeat at lunch.*
3. Peter didn't finish unloading the truck because John didn't help him.
4. Jack was late to his own wedding because his watch was ten minutes slow.
5. I don't ride the bus to work every morning because it's always so crowded.
6. I didn't bring extra money with me because you didn't tell me we were going to dinner after the movie.
7. Sam didn't know that highway 57 was closed, so he didn't take an alternative route.
8. Because I lost my key, I had to pound on the door to wake my roommate when I got home last night.

◇ PRACTICE 6—GUIDED STUDY: Conditional sentences. (Charts 10-1 → 10-4)

Directions: Make an "*if* clause" from the given information and then supply a "*result* clause" using your own words.

Example:
   I wasn't late to work yesterday.
   → *If I had been late to work yesterday, I would have missed the regular morning meeting.*

   Tom asked my permission before he took my bicycle.
   → *If Tom hadn't asked my permission before he took my bicycle, I would have been angry.*

1. I wasn't absent from class yesterday.
2. I don't have enough energy today.
3. Ocean water is salty.

4. Our teacher likes his/her job.

5. I don't know how to swim.

6. You didn't ask for my opinion.

7. Water is heavier than air.

8. Most nations support world trade agreements.

◇ **PRACTICE 7—GUIDED STUDY: Conditional sentences. (Charts 10-1 → 10-4)**

Directions: Make a true statement about the given topic. Then make a contrary-to-fact conditional sentence about that statement.

Examples:
yourself → *I am twenty years old. If I were seventy years old, I would already have lived most of my life.*
ice → *Ice doesn't sink. If the polar ice caps sank, the level of the oceans would rise and flood coastal cities.*

Topics:

1. yourself	5. peace	9. your activities right now
2. fire	6. vegetables	10. your activities last night
3. a member of your family	7. air	11. dinosaurs
4. a famous person	8. a member of this class	12. space travel

◇ **PRACTICE 8—SELFSTUDY: Using progressive forms and mixed time in conditional sentences. (Charts 10-5 and 10-6)**

Directions: Using the given information, complete the conditional sentences.

1. It is raining, so we won't finish the game.
   → If it _____*weren't raining*_____, we _____*would finish*_____ the game.

2. I didn't eat lunch and now I'm hungry.
   → If I _____*had eaten*_____ lunch, I _____*wouldn't be*_____ hungry now.

3. Bob left his wallet at home this morning, and now he doesn't have any money for lunch.
   → If Bob _____ his wallet at home this morning, he _____
   _____ some money for lunch now.

4. Carol didn't answer the phone because she was studying.
   → Carol _____ the phone if she _____.

5. The sun was shining, so we went to the beach yesterday.
   → If the sun _____, we _____ to the
   beach yesterday.

6. Every muscle in my body aches today because I played basketball for three hours last night.
   → Every muscle in my body _____ today if I _____
   _____ basketball for three hours last night.

7. Barry stops to shake everyone's hand because he's running for political office.
   → Barry _____ to shake everyone's hand if he _____
   _____ for political office.

8. We didn't eat all of the turkey at dinner last night, so we have to have turkey again tonight.

→ If we _____ all of the turkey at dinner last night, we

_____ turkey again tonight.

9. The music was playing loudly at the restaurant, so I didn't hear everything Mr. Lee said during dinner.

→ If the music _____ loudly, I _____

everything Mr. Lee said during dinner.

10. The library is closing now, so we'll have to leave before finishing our research.

→ If the library _____ now, we _____

before finishing our research.

◇ PRACTICE 9—SELFSTUDY: Using progressive forms and mixed time in conditional sentences. (Charts 10-5 and 10-6)

Directions: Using the given information, make conditional sentences. Use *if*.

1. The wind is blowing hard, so I won't take the boat out for a ride.
   → *If the wind weren't blowing hard, I would take the boat out for a ride.*

2. I feel better now because you talked to me about my problems last night.
   → *I wouldn't feel better now if you hadn't talked to me about my problems last night.*

3. Gary carried heavy furniture when he helped Ann move. His back hurts now.

4. Paul is working on two jobs right now, so he doesn't have time to help you with your remodeling.

5. I wasn't working at the restaurant last night. I didn't wait on your table.

6. Because Diane asked questions every time she didn't understand a problem, she has a good understanding of geometry now.

7. A bulldozer was blocking the road, so we didn't arrive on time.

8. She is exhausted today because she didn't get any sleep last night.

9. They weren't paying attention, so they didn't see the sign marking their exit from the highway.

10. The doctor doesn't really care about his patients. He didn't explain the medical procedure to me before surgery.

◇ PRACTICE 10—GUIDED STUDY: Using *could, might,* and *should* in conditional sentences. (Chart 10-7)

Directions: Complete the following conditional sentences.

Examples:
  Ann could have . . . if . . . .
  → *Ann could have made it to class on time if the bus hadn't been late.*

  I might have helped . . . if . . . .
  → *I might have helped you if you had asked me earlier.*

If you should need . . . please . . . .
→ *If you should need more information, please give me a call.*

1. The situation might improve if . . . .
2. If anyone should get injured during the race . . . .
3. I couldn't have fixed the bicycle if . . . .
4. Mr. Swanson might have hired you for the summer if . . . .
5. If you should arrive at the meeting before I do . . . .
6. Some of the research might have been lost if . . . .
7. It looks like the catastrophe could have been avoided if . . . .
8. We could still get out of this mess if . . . .
9. If you should happen to . . . please . . . .
10. I might have . . . if I had . . . .
11. All things considered, I might not have succeeded if . . . .
12. . . . could have avoided the problem if . . . .
13. If your car should break down on the highway . . . .
14. I might understand your problem better if . . . .
15. You could have gotten the job if . . . .
16. . . . could have . . . if she had . . . .
17. If I could . . . I would . . . .
18. If I could have . . . I would have . . . .

◇ **PRACTICE 11—SELFSTUDY: Omitting *if*. (Chart 10-8)**

Directions: Make sentences with the same meaning by omitting **if**.

1. *If you should need* more money, go to the bank before six o'clock.

    → _____**Should you need**_____ more money, go to the bank before six o'clock.

2. *If I were* you, I wouldn't do that.

    → _____**Were I**_____ you, I wouldn't do that.

3. *If they had realized* the danger, they would have done it differently.

    → _____**Had they realized**_____ the danger, they would have done it differently.

4. *If Alan had tried* to explain, I'm sure the professor would have given him another chance.

    → _____ to explain, I'm sure the professor would have given him

    another chance.

5. *If anyone should call,* would you please take a message?

    → _____, would you please take a message?

6. *If I were* your teacher, I would insist you do better work.

    → _____ your teacher, I would insist you do better work.

7. *If everyone had arrived* on time, none of these problems would have occurred.

    → _____ on time, none of these problems would have occurred.

8. *If the post office should close* before I get there, I'll mail your package in the morning.

    → _____ before I get there, I'll mail your package in the morning.

9. *If I had not opened* the door when I did, I wouldn't have seen you walk by.

→ _____ the door when I did, I wouldn't have seen you walk by.

10. *If she were* just a little older, I would start giving her driving lessons.

→ _____ just a little older, I would start giving her driving lessons.

11. *If you should change* your mind, please let me know immediately.

→ _____ your mind, please let me know immediately.

12. She would have gotten the job *if she had been* better prepared.

→ She would have gotten the job _____ better prepared.

◇ **PRACTICE 12—GUIDED STUDY: Omitting *if*. (Chart 10-8)**

Directions: Make sentences with the same meaning by omitting *if*.

1. If I were your age, I'd do things differently.
   → *Were I your age, I'd do things differently.*

2. If they had asked, I'd have had to tell them.
   → *Had they asked, I'd have had to tell them.*

3. If she were ever in trouble, I'd do anything I could to help her.

4. If Bob should show up, please give him my message.

5. If my uncle had stood up to sing, I'd have been embarrassed.

6. If you should hear the fire alarm, leave the building at once.

7. If I were the greatest scientist in the world, I still wouldn't be able to figure this out.

8. If you hadn't lent Jason your car, none of this would have happened.

9. If the president should question these figures, have him talk to the bookkeeper.

10. If my roommate had not mentioned your visit, I wouldn't have known about your new job.

◇ **PRACTICE 13—SELFSTUDY: Implied conditions. (Chart 10-9)**

Directions: Using the given information, complete the implied "*if* clauses."

1. I would have walked with you, but I twisted my ankle.

   → I would have walked with you if _____ **I hadn't twisted my ankle.** _____.

2. Sara's dad would have picked her up. However, I forgot to tell him that she needed a ride.

   → Sara's dad would have picked her up _____ **if I hadn't forgotten to tell him** _____
   _____ **that she needed a ride.** _____

3. I couldn't have made it without your help.

   → I couldn't have made it if _____

4. Carol: Why didn't Bob tell his boss about the problem?

   Alice: He would have gotten into a lot of trouble.

   → Bob would have gotten into trouble if _____

5. I opened the door slowly. Otherwise, I could have hit someone.

→ If _____, I could have hit someone.

6. The clerk would have bagged my groceries, but the woman behind me started yelling impatiently at him to check her out.

→ The clerk would have bagged my groceries if _____

7. I wanted everyone to know about it. Otherwise, I would have asked you to keep it to yourself.

→ If _____, I would have asked you to keep it to yourself.

8. Doug would have gone with me, but his boss wouldn't give him the time off.

→ Doug would have gone with me if _____

9. I would go back to the office and get your briefcase for you. However, the building is locked.

→ I would go back to the office and get your briefcase for you if _____

10. The business would never have gotten off the ground without Marge giving us the benefit of her expertise.

→ The business would never have gotten off the ground if _____

11. Sandra drove straight to the garage when the engine started making loud noises. Otherwise, she might have ended up stranded on the side of the road.

→ Sandra might have ended up stranded on the side of the road if _____

12. The cast had wanted to celebrate after the opening night's performance. However, the director made them all stay to rehearse some troublesome parts of the play.

→ If the director _____, they would have celebrated after the opening night's performance.

◇ **PRACTICE 14—SELFSTUDY: Conditional sentences. (Charts 10-1 → 10-9)**

Directions: Choose the correct completion.

1. If I could speak Spanish, I _____ next year studying in Mexico.
   A. would spend   B. would have spent   C. had spent   D. will spend

2. It would have been a much more serious accident _____ fast at the time.
   A. had she been driving   B. was she driving
   C. she had driven   D. she drove

3. "Can I borrow your car for this evening?"
   "Sure, but Nora's using it right now. If she _____ it back in time, you're welcome to borrow it."
   A. brought   B. would bring   C. will bring   D. brings

4. I didn't get home until well after midnight last night. Otherwise, I _____ your call.
   A. returned   B. had returned
   C. would return   D. would have returned

5. If energy _____ inexpensive and unlimited, many things in the world would be different.
   A. is   B. will be   C. were   D. would be

6. We _____ the game if we'd had a few more minutes.
   A. might have won   B. won   C. had won   D. will win

7. I _____ William with me if I had known you and he didn't get along with each other.
   A. hadn't brought   B. didn't bring
   C. wouldn't have brought   D. won't bring

8. The lecturer last night didn't know what he was talking about, but if Dr. Mason _____, I would have listened carefully.
   A. had been lecturing   B. was lecturing
   C. would lecture   D. lectured

9. If you _____ to my advice in the first place, you wouldn't be in this mess right now.
   A. listen   B. will listen   C. had listened   D. listened

10. _____ interested in that subject, I would try to learn more about it.
    A. Were I   B. Should I   C. I was   D. If I am

11. If I _____ the same problems you had as a child, I might not have succeeded in life as well as you have.
    A. have   B. would have   C. had had   D. should have

12. I _____ you sooner had someone told me you were in the hospital.
    A. would have visited   B. visited
    C. had visited   D. visit

13. _____ more help, I could call my neighbor.
    A. Needed   B. Should I need   C. I have needed   D. I should need

14. _____ then what I know today, I would have saved myself a lot of time and trouble over the years.
    A. Had I known   B. Did I know   C. If I know   D. If I would know

15. Do you think there would be less conflict in the world if all people _____ the same language?
    A. spoke   B. speak   C. had spoken   D. will speak

16. If you can give me one good reason for your acting like this, _____ this incident again.
    A. I will never mention   B. I never mention
    C. will I never mention   D. I don't mention

17. I didn't know you were asleep. Otherwise, I _____ so much noise when I came in.
    A. didn't make   B. wouldn't have made
    C. won't make   D. don't make

18. Unless you _____ all of my questions, I can't do anything to help you.
    A. answered   B. answer   C. would answer   D. are answering

19. Had you told me that this was going to happen, I _____ it.
    A. would never have believed   B. don't believe
    C. hadn't believed   D. can't believe

20. If Jake _____ to go on the trip, would you have gone?
    A. doesn't agree   B. didn't agree
    C. hadn't agreed   D. wouldn't agree

◇ **PRACTICE 15—GUIDED STUDY: Expressing conditions. (Charts 10-1 → 10-9)**

Directions: Using the given information, make conditional sentences using "*if* clauses." Make two or more conditional sentences about each of the situations described below.

Example: Jan is working for a law firm, but she has been trying to find a different job for a long time. She doesn't like her job at the law firm. Recently she was offered a job with a computer company closer to her home. She wanted to accept it, but the salary was too low.
→ *If Jan liked her job at the law firm, she wouldn't be trying to find a different job.*
→ *Jan would have accepted the job at the computer company if the salary hadn't been too low.*

1. Jim: Why don't we go to the ball game after work today?
   Ron: I'd like to but I can't.
   Jim: Why not?
   Ron: I have a dinner meeting with a client.
   Jim: Well, maybe some other time.

2. Tommy had a pet mouse. He took it to school. His friend, Jimmy, took the mouse and put it in the teacher's desk drawer. When the teacher found the mouse, she jumped in surprise and tried to kill it with a book. Tommy ran to the front of the room and saved his pet mouse. Tommy got into a lot of trouble with his teacher.

3. My brother and I rented a truck and loaded up all of my furniture to move across town. I was driving the truck. When I heard something crashing around in the back, I turned around and, at that moment, went through a red light and crashed into a police car. Repairs to the truck and police car, the fine for breaking the law, and the damage to the furniture all cost a lot of money. In short, it would have been a lot less expensive to hire professional movers to take everything to the new house.

4. My ax was broken, and I wanted to borrow my neighbor's so that I could chop some wood. Then I remembered that I had already borrowed his saw and never returned it. I have since lost the saw, and I'm too embarrassed to tell him. Because of that, I decided not to ask him for his ax.

◇ **PRACTICE 16—GUIDED STUDY: Conditional Sentences. (Charts 10-1 → 10-9)**

Directions: Using the given ideas, make conditional sentences.

Examples:

    rain last Saturday/go (somewhere)
    → *If it hadn't been raining last Saturday, we could have gone on a picnic.*

    be a magician/make (something/someone) disappear
    → *If I were a magician, I could make rabbits disappear into thin air.*

    eat properly/run out of energy
    → *If I don't eat properly during the day, I always run out of energy late in the afternoon.*

1. know the answer/tell you
2. come to my house/cook dinner
3. be a teacher/teach
4. see a dragon/(do something)
5. be no fresh water/live
6. panic/die
7. listen/understand
8. score/win
9. make reservations/request a table for four
10. bus drivers be on strike/take a taxi
11. be no electricity/cook dinner
12. live in the city/raise horses
13. ten years old again/not have to (do something)
14. be a famous author/write about (something)
15. sit next to any famous person of my choosing on an airplane/sit next to (someone)

◇ **PRACTICE 17—GUIDED STUDY: Conditional sentences. (Charts 10-1 → 10-9)**

Directions: Answer the following questions.

1. If you could have free service for the rest of your life from a chauffeur, cook, housekeeper, or gardener, which would you choose? Why?

2. If you had to leave your country and build a new life elsewhere, where would you go? Why?

3. If you had control of all medical research in the world and, by concentrating funds and efforts, could find the cure to only one disease in the next 25 years, which disease would you select? Why?

4. If you could stay one particular age for a span of 50 years, what age would you choose? Why? (At the end of the 50 years, you would suddenly turn 50 years older.)

5. You have promised to spend an evening with your best friend. Then you discover you have the chance to spend the evening with _____ (*supply the name of a famous person*). Your friend is not invited. What would you do? Why?

6. Assume that you have a good job. If your boss told you to do something that you think is wrong, would you do it? Why or why not? You understand that if you don't do it, you will lose your job.

7. If you had to choose among good health, a loving family, and wealth (and you could have only one of the three during the rest of your life), which would you choose? Why?

8. Under what conditions, if any, would you . . .
    a. exceed the speed limit while driving?
    b. lie to your best friend?
    c. disobey an order from your boss?
    d. steal food?
    e. carry a friend on your back for a long distance?
    f. not pay your rent?
    g. (*make up other conditions for your classmates to discuss*)

◇ PRACTICE 18—SELFSTUDY: Using *wish*. (Charts 10-10 and 10-11)

Directions: Using the information in parentheses, complete the sentences.

1. (The sun isn't shining.) I wish the sun _____*were shining*_____ right now.

2. (I wanted you to go.) I wish you _____*had gone*_____ with us to the concert last night.

3. (John didn't drive.) I wish John _____ to work. I'd ask him for a ride home.

4. (I can't swim.) I wish I _____ so that I would feel safe in a boat.

5. (I want you to stop fighting.) I wish you _____ fighting and try to work things out.

6. (I wanted to win.) I wish we _____ the game last night.

7. (Bill didn't get the promotion.) I wish Bill _____ the promotion. He feels bad.

8. (I quit my job.) I wish I _____ my job until I'd found another one.

9. (It isn't winter.) I wish it _____ winter so that I could go skiing.

10. (I want Al to sing.) I wish Al _____ a couple of songs. He has a good voice.

11. (Diane can't bring her children.) I wish Diane _____ her children with her tomorrow. They would be good company for mine.

12. (No one offered to help.) I wish someone _____ to help us find our way when we got lost in the middle of the city.

◇ PRACTICE 19—SELFSTUDY: Using *wish*. (Charts 10-10 and 10-11)

Directions: Complete the sentences with the words in parentheses.

1. Tom's in trouble with the teacher. Now he wishes he (*miss, not*) _____*had not missed*_____ class three times this week.

2. A: It's raining. I wish it (*stop*) _____*would stop*_____.

   B: Me too. I wish the sun (*shine*)_____*were shining*_____ so that we could go swimming.

3. A: Alice doesn't like her job as a nurse. She wishes she (*go, not*) _____ to nursing school.

   B: Really? What does she wish she (*study*) _____ instead of nursing?

4. I wish I (*move, not*) _____ to this town. I can't seem to make any friends, and everything is so congested. I wish I (*take*) _____ the job I was offered in the small town near here.

5. I know I should quit smoking. I wish you (*stop*) _____ nagging me about it.

6. A: Did you get your car back from the garage?

   B: Yes, and it still isn't fixed. I wish I (*pay, not*) _____ them in full when I picked up the car. I should have waited to be sure that everything was all right.

7. A: I wish you (hurry) _____! We're going to be late.

   B: I wish you (relax) _____. We've got plenty of time.

8. I wish you (invite, not) _____ the neighbors over for dinner when you talked to them this afternoon. I don't feel like cooking a big dinner.

9. A: I know that something's bothering you. I wish you (tell) _____ me what it is. Maybe I can help you.

   B: I appreciate it, but I can't discuss it now.

10. A: My feet are killing me! I wish I (wear) _____ more comfortable shoes.

    B: Yeah, me too. I wish I (realize) _____ that we were going to have to walk this much.

11. A: How do you like the new president of our association?

    B: Not much. I wish he (elect, not) _____. I never should have voted for him.

    A: Oh, really? Then you probably wish I (vote, not) _____ for him. If you recall, he won by only one vote. You and I could have changed the outcome of the election if we'd known then what we know now.

12. A: I wish we (buy) _____ everything we wanted all the time.

    B: In that case, you probably wish money (grow) _____ on trees. We'd plant some in the back yard, and just go out and pick a little from the branches every morning.

13. A: My thirteen-year-old daughter wishes she (be, not) _____ so tall and wishes her hair (be) _____ black and straight.

    B: Really? My daughter wishes she (be) _____ taller and that her hair (be) _____ blond and curly.

14. A: I wish most world leaders (meet) _____ in the near future and reach some agreement on environmental issues. I'm worried the earth is running out of time.

    B:. I wish I (disagree) _____ with you and (prove) _____ your fears groundless, but I'm afraid you might be right.

◇ PRACTICE 20—GUIDED STUDY: Using *wish*. (Charts 10-10 and 10-11)

Directions: Using the given ideas, make sentences with **wish**. Add something that explains why you are making this wish.

Examples:
  be different → *I wish my name were different. I've never liked having "Daffodil" as my first name.*
  go to the moon → *I wish I could go to the moon for a vacation. It would be fun to be able to leap long distances, given the moon's lower gravity.*

1. be different
2. know several world leaders personally
3. speak every language in the world
4. be more patient and understanding
5. interview some great people in history
6. travel by instant teleportation
7. remember everything I read
8. be a big movie star
9. read people's minds
10. be born in the last century

◇ PRACTICE 21—SELFSTUDY: *As if/as though.* (Chart 10-12)

Directions: Using the information in parentheses, complete the sentences.

1. Tim acts as if he _____*were*_____ the boss. (Tim isn't the boss.)
2. This hole in my shirt looks as if it __*had been made*__ by a bullet. (The hole wasn't made by a bullet.)
3. Barbara looked at me as though she _____ never _____ me before. (She has met me many times before.)
4. They treat their dog as if it _____ a child. (The dog isn't a child.)
5. She went right on talking as though she _____ a word I'd said. (She heard everything I said.)
6. You look so depressed. You look as if you _____ a friend in the world. (You have many friends.)
7. He looked right through me as if I _____. (I exist.)
8. Craig bumped the other car and then continued as though nothing _____. (Something happened.)
9. A: Have Joe and Diane ever met?
   B: I don't think so. Why?
   A: He came in and started talking to her as if they _____ old friends. (They aren't old friends.)
10. I can hear his voice so clearly that it's as if he _____ here in this room. (He isn't here in this room; he's next door.)
11. It was so quiet that it seemed as if the earth _____. (The earth didn't stop.)
12. I turned, and there she was. It was as though she _____ out of nowhere. (She didn't appear out of nowhere.)

◇ PRACTICE 22—GUIDED STUDY: *As if/as though.* (Chart 10-12)

Directions: Complete the sentences with your own words.

Examples:
   When I walked into the room, I felt as though . . . .
   → *When I walked into the room, I felt as though everyone were staring at me.*

   I got angry at Mary. She talked to me as if . . . .
   → *I got angry at Mary. She talked to me as if I were a small child who needed discipline.*

1. Are you tired? You look as if . . . .
2. George only recently started piano lessons, but he plays as if . . . .
3. He's not very knowledgeable on the subject, but he speaks as though . . . .
4. Richard is very confident. He walks around as though . . . .

5. This meat is terrible. It tastes as if . . . .

6. You're looking at me as if . . . .

7. Bob is extremely pale. He looks as if . . . .

8. He's acting so nonchalant, as though . . . .

9. After he got knocked over, he got up as if . . . .

10. The child innocently whistled and looked around as though . . . .

◇ **PRACTICE 23—GUIDED STUDY: Conditionals. (Charts 10-1 → 10-12)**

Directions: Complete the sentences with the words in parentheses.

TOM: What's wrong, Bob? You look awful! You look as if you (*1. run*) _____

over by a truck!

BOB: Well, you (*2. look*) _____ this bad today, too, if you (*3. have*)

_____ a day like mine yesterday. My car slid into a tree because the

roads were icy.

TOM: Oh? I was driving on the icy roads yesterday, and I didn't slide into a tree. What happened?

BOB: Well, I suppose if I (*4. drive, not*) _____ so fast, I (*5. slide, not*)

_____ into the tree.

TOM: Icy roads and speed don't mix. If drivers (*6. step*) _____ on the gas on

ice, they're likely to spin their car in a circle.

BOB: I know! And not only is my car a mess now, but I didn't have my driver's license with me, so

now I'll have to pay an extra fine when I go to court next month.

TOM: Why were you driving without your license?

BOB: Well, I lost my wallet a few days ago. It slipped out of my pocket while I was riding the bus

to work.

TOM: What a tale of woe! If you (*7. take, not*) _____ that bus, you (*8. lose,

not*) _____ your wallet. If you (*9. lose, not*) _____

your wallet, you (*10. have*) _____ your driver's license with you when

you hit a tree. If you (*11. have*) _____ your license with you, you (*12.

have to pay, not*) _____ a big fine when you go to court next week. And

of course, if you (*13. drive, not*) _____ too fast, you (*14. run into, not*)

_____ a tree, and you (*15. be, not*) _____ in this

mess now. If I (*16. be*) _____ you, I (*17. take*) _____

it easy for a while and just (*18. stay*) _____ home where you're safe and

sound.

BOB: Enough about me! How about you?

TOM: Well, things are really looking up for me. I'm planning to take off for Florida as soon as I finish my finals. I'm sick of all this cold, rainy weather we've been having. I (*19. stay*) _____ here for vacation if the weather (*20. be, not*) _____ so bad. But I need some sun!

BOB: I wish I (*21. go*) _____ with you. How are you planning on getting there?

TOM: If I have enough money, I (*22. fly*) _____. Otherwise, I (*23. take*) _____ the bus. I wish I (*24. drive*) _____ my own car there because it (*25. be*) _____ nice to have it to drive around in once I get there, but it's such a long trip. I've been looking for a friend to go with me and share the driving.

BOB: Hey, I have a super idea. Why don't I go with you? I can share the driving. I'm a great driver!

TOM: Didn't you just get through telling me that you'd wrapped your car around a tree?

◇ **PRACTICE TEST A—SELFSTUDY: Conditional sentences. (Chapter 10)**

Directions: Choose the correct answer.

Example:
If I __C__ you, I would get some rest before the game tomorrow.
   A. am   *B. could be*   *C. were*   *D. had been*

1. When I stopped talking, Sam finished my sentence for me as though he _____ my mind.
   A. would read   B. had read   C. reads   D. can read

2. If you _____, I would have brought my friends over to your house this evening to watch TV, but I didn't want to bother you.
   A. had studied   B. studied
   C. hadn't been studying   D. didn't study

3. I wish I _____ you some money for your rent, but I'm broke myself.
   A. can lend   B. would lend   C. could lend   D. will lend

4. If someone _____ into the store, smile and say, "May I help you?"
   A. comes   B. came   C. would come   D. could come

5. "Are we lost?"
   "I think so. I wish we _____ a map with us today."
   A. were bringing   B. brought   C. had brought   D. would bring

6. "Here's my phone number."
   "Thanks. I'll give you a call if I _____ some help tomorrow."
   A. will need   B. need   C. would need   D. needed

7. If I weren't working for an accounting firm, I _____ in a bank.
   A. work   B. will work   C. have worked   D. would be working

8. Ed invested a lot of money with a dishonest advisor, and lost nearly all of it. Now he is having serious financial problems. He _____ in this position if he had listened to some of his friends.
   A. will be   B. wouldn't be   C. will be   D. hadn't been

9. The world _____ a better place if we had known a hundred years ago what we know today about the earth's environment.
   A. will be   B. was   C. should be   D. might be

10. The medicine made me feel dizzy. I felt as though the room _____ around and around.
    A. were spinning   B. will spin
    C. spins   D. would be spinning

11. "I'm really sorry about what happened during the meeting. I felt I had no choice."
    "It's okay. I'm sure you wouldn't have done it if you _____."
    A. should have   B. had to
    C. hadn't had to   D. have to

12. _____ you, I'd think twice about that decision. It could be a bad move.
    A. If I had been   B. Were I
    C. Should I be   D. If I am

13. "Was Pam seriously injured in the automobile accident?"
    "She broke her arm. It _____ much worse if she hadn't been wearing her seat belt."
    A. will be   B. would have been   C. was   D. were

14. If my candidate had won the election, I _____ happy now.
    A. am   B. would be   C. was   D. can be

15. I wish Janet _____ to the meeting this afternoon.
    A. came   B. will come   C. can come   D. could come

16. I _____ you to the woman I was speaking with, but I couldn't think of her name.
    A. will introduce   B. would introduce
    C. would have introduced   D. couldn't have introduced

17. "What _____ today if you hadn't come here this weekend?"
    "I guess I'd be putting in extra hours at my office."
    A. did you do   B. can you do   C. will you be doing   D. would you be doing

18. Page 12 of the manual that came with the appliance says, "_____ any problem with the merchandise, contact your local dealer."
    A. You should have   B. Do you have
    C. Had you have   D. Should you have

19. Marge walked away from the discussion. Otherwise, she _____ something she would regret later.
    A. will say   B. said   C. might say   D. might have said

20. I would never have encouraged you to go into this field _____ it would be so stressful for you. I'm sorry it's been so difficult for you.
    A. had I known   B. and I had known
    C. should I know   D. but I knew

◇ PRACTICE TEST B—GUIDED STUDY: Conditional sentences. (Chapter 10)

Directions: Choose the correct answer.

Example:
If I __C__ you, I would get some rest before the game tomorrow.
   A. am   *B. could be*   *C. were*   *D. had been*

1. Please keep your voice down in this section of the library. If you _____ to talk loudly, I will have to ask you to leave.
   A. continued   B. could continue   C. will continue   D. continue

2. Gloria never seems to get tired. I sure wish I _____ her energy.
    A. would have   B. have   C. have had   D. had

3. "Why didn't Bill get the promotion he was expecting?"
   "He may not be qualified. If he were, he _____ that promotion last year."
    A. would have been given   B. were given
    C. would be given   D. was given

4. If I could find Rob's phone number, I _____ him about the change in plans. Maybe somebody
   else will call him.
    A. called   B. had called   C. could call   D. will call

5. "How do you like your new apartment?"
   "The apartment itself is great, but I wish I _____ used to the constant noise from the street
   below."
    A. got   B. could get
    C. had gotten   D. am

6. I was very engrossed in that presentation on Australia. The video tapes were so realistic that it
   was as though we _____ there, driving through the outback country.
    A. were   B. have been   C. are   D. will be

7. If I _____ following that other car too closely, I would have been able to stop in time instead of
   running into it.
    A. wasn't   B. would have been   C. was   D. hadn't been

8. "Why aren't you going mountain climbing with the rest of us next weekend?"
   "To be honest with you, I'm a coward. If I were brave, I _____ with you."
    A. would have gone   B. would go
    C. go   D. will go

9. "Will you see Tom at lunch today? I'd like you to give him a message for me."
   "I'm not going to lunch, but if I _____ him later, I'll give him your message."
    A. should see   B. will see   C. would see   D. could see

10. I'm really sleepy today. I wish I _____ Bob to the airport late last night.
    A. didn't have to take   B. weren't taking
    C. hadn't had to take   D. didn't take

11. Hurry! We've got to leave the house immediately. Otherwise, _____ the opening ceremony.
    A. we'd miss   B. we'd have missed
    C. we miss   D. we're going to miss

12. "Why didn't you tell me you were having so many problems?"
    "I _____ you, but I figured you had enough to worry about without my problems, so I said
    nothing."
    A. would tell   B. would have told   C. would be telling   D. had told

13. A nation's balance of trade is considered unfavorable if it _____ more money on imports than
    it gains from exports.
    A. will spend   B. would spend   C. can spend   D. spends

14. Many people who live near nuclear plants are concerned. _____ go wrong, the impact on the
    surrounding area could be disastrous.
    A. Something would   B. Something will
    C. Should something   D. Does something

15. Had I known the carpenter was going to take three days to show up, I _____ the materials and
    done the work myself. It would be finished by now.
    A. will get   B. would have gotten   C. might get   D. will have gotten

16. I wish you _____ making that noise. It's bothering me.
    A. would stop   B. are going to stop   C. stop   D. can stop

17. A huge tree crashed through the bedroom roof and broke my bed and most of the other furniture. _____ in the room, I would have been killed.
    A. Should I be   B. Had I been   C. Would I have been   D. Would I be

18. If everyone _____, how would we control air traffic? Surely, we'd all be crashing into each other.
    A. can fly   B. will fly   C. flies   D. could fly

19. If the world's tropical forests continue to disappear at their present rate, many animal species _____ extinct.
    A. became   B. would have become C. will become   D. would become

20. When my lost briefcase was returned with my year-long research results intact, I felt tremendously relieved. It was as if a huge and heavy weight _____ from my shoulders.
    A. had been lifted   B. is being lifted
    C. would be lifted   D. is lifting

 *Answer Key*

WORKBOOK B
UNDERSTANDING AND USING ENGLISH GRAMMAR, SECOND EDITION

Answers to the Selfstudy Practices

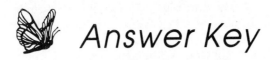

Answer Key

WORKBOOK B
UNDERSTANDING AND USING ENGLISH GRAMMAR, SECOND EDITION

Answers to the Selfstudy Practices

To the student: To make it easy to correct your own answers, remove this answer key along the perforations and make a separate answer key booklet for yourself.

Chapter 5: SINGULAR AND PLURAL

◇ **1 (p. 157):** 1. cares...feathers   2. occupations...Doctors...Pilots...airplanes...Farmers... crops...Shepherds   3. designs...buildings...digs...objects   4. computers... computers   5. factories...employs   6. Kangaroos...animals...continents...zoos 7. Mosquitos/Mosquitoes   8. tomatoes   9. Birds...insects...mammals... forms...characteristics   10. creatures...five senses...these senses...Birds... Animals...dogs...human beings

◇ **2 (p. 158):** 1. men   2. boxes...oxen   3. teeth   4. matches   5. mice   6. potatoes 7. beaches...cliffs   8. leaves   9. attorneys   10. discoveries...laboratories 11. fish   12. wolves...foxes...deer...sheep   13. children...bushes 14. ducks...geese   15. echoes   16. pianos

◇ **3 (p. 159):** 1. theses   2. phenomena   3. hypotheses   4. crises   5. memoranda   6. media 7. criteria   8. curricula   9. stimuli   10. bacteria   11. oases   12. data

◇ **4 (p. 159):** 1. friends'   2. friend's   3. father's   4. aunts'...mother's   5. aunt's 6. astronauts'   7. children's   8. child's   9. secretary's   10. people's   11. Bill's 12. Bess's (OR: Bess')   13. diplomats'   14. diplomat's

◇ **5 (p. 160):** 1. Mary's father...He's a dentist.   **2.** Jack's parents live...His parents' home   3. Our teacher's last name...She's one of the best teachers   4. Our teachers' last names... They're all good teachers.   5. Ms. Wells' (OR: Wells's) husband...Ms. Hunt's husband 6. It's well known that a bear likes   7. Ann's telephone number [NOTE: No apostrophes are used with possessive pronouns (e.g., *hers, ours*). See Appendix 1, Chart A-7.]   8. Although it's found...our children's and grandchildren's lives....

◇ **7 (p. 161):** 1. They sell **shoes**...a **shoe** store   2. I like **tomato** salads...contain **tomatoes**   3. from black **beans**...black **bean** soup   4. for **babies**...**baby** food   5. a **vegetable** garden... kinds of **vegetables**   6. addicted to **drugs**...**drug** addicts   7. from **mosquitoes/ mosquitos**...a **mosquito** net   8. for **salads**...a **salad** fork

◇ **8 (p. 162):** 1. a **two-hour** wait . . . for **two hours**   2. is **ten years old** . . . a **ten-year-old** brother   3. had only **two lanes** . . . a **two-lane** highway   4. a **five-minute** speech . . . for **five minutes**   5. a **sixty-year-old** house . . . is **sixty years old**   6. **ten** different **speeds** . . . a **ten-speed** bike   7. won **six games** . . . a **six-game** winning streak   8. **three-letter** words . . . has **three letters**

◇ **9 (p. 162):** 1. a bank robber   2. a bullfighter   3. a stamp collector   4. an animal trainer   5. a storyteller   6. a tax collector   7. a can opener   8. a windshield wiper   9. a wage earner   10. an office manager   11. a computer programmer   12. a bookkeeper   13. a spot remover   14. a pot holder   15. a troublemaker   16. a mind reader   17. a hair dryer (OR: hair drier)   18. a potato peeler   19. a tennis player   20. a firefighter   21. a mail carrier

◇ **10 (p. 163):** 1. **A** bird   2. **An** animal   3. **Ø** Food   4. **A** concert   5. **An** opera   6. **Ø** Music   7. **A** cup   8. **Ø** Milk   9. **An** island   10. **Ø** Gold   11. **A** bridge   12. **A** valley   13. **Ø** Health   14. **An** adjective   15. **Ø** Knowledge   16. **Ø** Gold   17. **A** professional golfer   18. **A** tree   19. **Ø** Water   20. **Ø** Homework   21. **Ø** Grammar   22. **A** sentence   23. **Ø** English   24. **A** leaf   25. **An** orange   26. **Ø** Fruit   27. **Ø** Iron   28. **An** iron   29. **A** basketball   30. **Ø** Basketball

◇ **11 (p. 164):** 1. **an** announcement   2. **a** bird   3. **some** birds   4. **some** money   5. **an** accident   6. **some** homework   7. **a** table   8. **some** furniture   9. **some** chairs   10. **some** advice   11. **a** suitcase   12. **some** luggage   13. **an** earthquake   14. **some** letters   15. **a** letter   16. **some** mail   17. **a** machine   18. **some** new machinery   19. **Some** machines   20. **some** junk   21. **an** old basket   22. **some** old boots

◇ **13 (p. 165):** 1. [*no change*] . . . eyes   2. [*no change*]   3. [*no change*]   4. sandwiches   5. [*no change*]   6. [*no change*]   7. photographs   8. [*no change*]   9. ideas   10. [*no change*]   11. [*no change*]   12. [*no change*]   13. words   14. [*no change*]   15. [*no change*]   16. [*no change*]   17. gloves   18. cars . . . minutes . . . [*no change*]   19. [*no changes in whole sentence*]   20. [*only one change*]: customs

◇ **15 (p. 166):** 1. many cities   2. much money   3. is too much furniture   4. aren't many hotels   5. much mail   6. many letters   7. isn't much traffic   8. aren't many cars   9. much work   10. many sides [*Answer: A pentagon has five sides.*]   11. much information   12. much homework   13. many people   14. much postage   15. is too much violence   16. much patience   17. many patients   18. many teeth [*Answer: The average person has 32 teeth.*]   19. isn't much international news   20. many fish are   21. many continents are [*Answer: There are 7 continents: Africa, Antarctica, Asia, Australia, Europe, North America, and South America.*]   22. much progress

◇ **16 (p. 167):**

1. lamps	4. Ø	7. sleep	10. patience
Ø	loaves of bread	information	wealth
Ø	Ø	facts	Ø
necklaces	jars of honey	help	Ø
2. Ø	5. novels	8. women	11. luck
salt	Ø	movies	money
equipment	poems	scenes	advice
Ø	Ø	Ø	Ø
3. stamps	6. orange juice	9. shirts	12. ideas
rice	light bulbs	Ø	theories
stuff	hardware	pens	hypotheses
things	computer software	Ø	Ø

◇ **17 (p. 168):** 1. a little   2. (very) few   3. A little   4. (very) little   5. a few   6. (very) few   7. a few   8. a little   9. (very) little   10. a little   11. a few   12. (Very) Few

◇ **18 (p. 169):** 1. Ø   2. of   3. Ø   4. of   5. Ø   6. of   7. of   8. Ø   9. Ø   10. of   11. Ø   12. Ø   13. of   14. Ø   15. of   16. Ø   17. Ø   18. of OR: Ø   19. of OR: Ø   20. Ø   21. of   22. Ø   23. Ø...Ø   24. of   25. Ø   26. Ø   27. of   28. Ø   29. Ø   30. of

◇ **21 (p. 171):** 1. student   2. students   3. room   4. rooms   5. window   6. windows   7. item   8. items   9. country   10. countries   11. person   12. question   13. children... child   14. problems   15. applicants

◇ **23 (p. 172):** 1. are   2. vote   3. have   4. was   5. leads   6. consists   7. is   8. Isn't   9. speak and understand   10. are   11. do   12. are   13. have   14. continues   15. confirms   16. is...is   17. are   18. were   19. is   20. was   21. contain   22. Are   23. is   24. are [*Answer: The population of Canada is over 27 million.*]   25. is   26. begin [*Answer: Four (Alabama, Alaska, Arkansas, and Arizona).*]   27. is [*Answer: Antarctica is the only uninhabited continent.*]   28. is [*Answer: Approximately 3% of all the water in the world is fresh water.*]   29. is   30. have [*Answer: The only places in the world where snakes do not live are New Zealand, Ireland, the North Pole, the South Pole, and a few islands in the South Pacific.*]

◇ **25 (p. 175):** 1. his/her; his or her; his   2. their   3. their   4. his/her; his or her; his   5. his/her; his or her; his; her   6. their   7. them OR: him/her   8. their OR: his/her; his or her; his; her   9. Their   10. They have...they   11. They   12. It was

◇ **26 (p. 175):** 1. himself   2. myself   3. himself   4. yourself   5. yourselves   6. themselves   7. myself   8. themselves   9. myself   10. herself   11. himself   12. yourself   13. ourselves   14. myself   15. himself

◇ **27 (p. 177):** 1. ourselves...we are...our   2. yourself...you are...your   3. yourselves...you are...your   4. themselves...they are...their   5. INFORMAL: themselves...they are...their/FORMAL: himself...he is...his OR: herself...she is...her (*Also possible*: him/herself...s/he is...his/her)

◇ **29 (p. 178):** 1. another   2. Others   3. The other   4. another   5. the others   6. the other [*Answer: The other states are Oregon, California, Hawaii, and Alaska.*]   7. other   8. others...others...Other   9. another   10. another   11. the others   12. other

◇ **32 (p. 180):**
1. In my country, there **are** a **lot** of [OR: are **lots** of] schools.
2. Writing compositions **is** very hard for me.
3. The front-page articles in the daily newspaper **have** the most important news.
4. Besides the zoo and the art museum, I have visited many **other** places in this city.
5. It's difficult for me to understand English when people **use** a lot of **slang**.
6. **Students**... and hand in **their** assignments on time. [OR: **A student**... and hand in **his/her** assignments on time.]
7. In the past, horses **were** the principal **means** of transportation.
8. In my opinion, [Ø] **English** is **an** easy language to learn.
9. There **are** many different **kinds** of **animals** in the world.
10. They want to move to **another** city because they don't like [Ø] cold weather.
11. I like to travel because I like to learn about other **countries** and **customs**.
12. Collecting stamps is one of my **hobbies**.
13. Chicago has many tall **skyscrapers**.
14. I came here three and a half **months** ago. I think I have made [Ø] good progress in English.
15. I was looking for my clothes, but I couldn't find **them**.

1. C   2. D   3. A   4. C   5. C   6. B   7. B   8. C   9. A
10. C   11. A   12. A   13. D   14. A   15. A   16. B   17. C   18. D
19. D   20. B

Chapter 6: ADJECTIVE CLAUSES

◇ **1 (p. 185):**   1. a. that are marked with a small red dot . . .   b. which are marked with a small red dot
2. a. who sits at the first desk on the right . . .   b. that sits at the first desk on the right
3. a. that I bought . . .   b. which I bought . . .   c. I bought   4. a. that I met at the
meeting . . .   b. who(m) I met at the meeting . . .   c. I met at the meeting   5. a. we listened
to last night . . .   b. that we listened to last night . . .   c. which we listened to last night . . .
d. to which we listened last night   6. a. I told you about . . .   b. who(m) I told you
about . . .   c. that I told you about . . .   d. about whom I told you   7. whose parents you
just met   8. who played at the concert last night   9. a waiter has to serve at a restaurant
10. Bob recommended   11. whose book on time and space has been translated into dozens
of languages   12. who lives next door to us

◇ **2 (p. 186):**   1. who(m)/that/Ø   2. who/that   3. which/that/Ø   4. which   5. who(m)/that/Ø
6. who/that   7. whose   8. whom   9. which/that

◇ **3 (p. 187):**   1. which/that   2. who/that   3. which/that   4. which/that   5. who/that
6. which/that/Ø   7. who(m)/that/Ø   8. which/that/Ø   9. which   10. which/that/Ø
11. whom   12. who(m)/that/Ø

◇ **4 (p. 188):**   1. Louis knows the woman **who/that is meeting us at the airport.**
2. The chair **which/that/Ø Sally inherited from her grandmother** is an antique.
3. The bench **which/that/Ø I sat on** was wet./The bench **on which I sat** was wet.
4. The man **who(m)/that/Ø I hired to paint my house** finished the job in four days.
5. I miss seeing the old woman **who/that used to sell flowers on that street corner.**
6. The architect **who(m)/that/Ø Mario works with** is brilliant./The architect **with whom
Mario works** is brilliant.
7. Mary tutors students **who/that need extra help in geometry.**
8. I took a picture of the rainbow **which/that appeared in the sky after the shower.**

◇ **5 (p. 189):**   1. I spoke to the man whose wife had been admitted to the hospital.
2. I read about a child whose life was saved by her pet dog.
3. The students whose names were called raised their hands.
4. Jack knows a man whose name is William Blueheart Duckbill, Jr.
5. The police came to question the woman whose purse was stolen outside the supermarket.
6. We live in a small town whose inhabitants are almost invariably friendly and helpful.
7. The day care center was established to take care of children whose parents work . . . .
8. We couldn't find the person whose car was blocking our driveway.
9. Tobacco is a plant whose large leaves are used for smoking or chewing.
10. The professor told the three students whose reports were turned in late that he would
accept the late papers this time but never again.

◇ **6 (p. 189):**   1. A,D   2. B,C,D   3. C,D   4. B   5. D   6. B,C   7. A   8. C,D
9. B,C,D   10. B   11. A   12. A

◇ **7 (p. 190):**   1. speak   2. speaks   3. are . . . don't   4. offers . . . are   5. measures . . . walks
6. suffer   7. were   8. have   9. have   10. work   11. are   12. state . . . wish

◇ **8 (p. 190):** 1. In our village, there were many people **who/that** didn't have much money. OR: In our village, many people didn't have much money.   2. I enjoyed the book that you told me to read (*omit "it"*).   3. I still remember the man who (*omit "he"*) taught me to play the violin when I was a boy.   4. I showed my father a picture of the car I am going to buy (*omit "it"*) as soon as I save enough money.   5. The woman about **whom** I was talking (*omit "about"*) suddenly walked into the room. OR: The woman **who(m)/that/Ø** I was talking about suddenly....   6. Almost all of the people **who/that** appear on television wear makeup.   7. My grandfather was a community leader whom everyone in our town admired (*omit "him"*) very much.   8. I don't like to spend time with people **who/that** lose (*omit final "-s"*) their tempers easily.   9. I sit next to a person **whose** name is Ahmed.   10. In one corner of the marketplace, **there was** an old man who was playing a violin. OR: In one corner of the marketplace, an old man (*omit "who"*) was playing a violin.

◇ **9 (p. 191):** 1. That is the place **where** the accident occurred.   2. There was a time **when** movies cost a dime.   3. A cafe is a small restaurant **where** people can get a light meal.   4. Every neighborhood in Brussels has small cafes **where** customers drink coffee and eat pastries.   5. There was a time **when** dinosaurs dominated the earth.   6. The house **where** I was born and grew up was destroyed in an earthquake ten years ago.   7. Summer is the time of year **when** the weather is the hottest.   8. The miser hid his money in a place **where** it was safe from robbers.   9. There came a time **when** the miser had to spend his money.   10. ... so Dan took it back to the store **where** he'd bought it.

◇ **12 (p. 192):** 1. NO   2. YES... Paul O'Grady, who died two years ago, was a kind and loving man.   3. NO   4. YES... I made an appointment with Dr. Raven, who is considered an expert on eye disorders.   5. NO   6. NO   7. YES... Bogota, which is the capital of Colombia, is a cosmopolitan city.   8. YES... They climbed Mount Rainier, which is in the state of Washington, twice last year.   9. YES... Emeralds, which are valuable gemstones, are mined in Colombia.   10. YES... The company offered the position to John, whose department performed best this year.   11. YES... On our trip to Africa we visited Nairobi, which is near several fascinating game reserves, and then traveled to Egypt to see the pyramids.   12. NO   13. NO   14. YES... Larry was very close to his only brother, who was a famous social historian.   15. NO   16. NO   17. YES... A typhoon, which is a violent tropical storm, can cause great destruction.   18. NO

◇ **13 (p. 193):** 1. A   2. A,D   3. C   4. A   5. A,B,D,E   6. B   7. A   8. C   9. A,D   10. A   11. A,D   12. A   13. C,D,E

◇ **14 (p. 194):** 1. a   2. b   3. a   4. b   5. b   6. a   7. b   8. a

◇ **15 (p. 194):** 1. YES... Thirty people, two of whom were members of the crew, were killed in the ferry accident.   2. NO   3. YES... Over 500 students took the entrance examination, the results of which will be posted in the administration building at the end of the month.   4. YES... My instructor assigned 150 pages of reading for tomorrow, which is too much. I won't have time to do it.   5. NO   6. YES... The Caspian Sea, which is bounded by the Soviet Union and Iran, is fed by eight rivers.   7. YES... The supervisor was not happy with his work crew, none of whom seemed interested in doing quality work.   8. YES... My oldest brother, in whose house I lived for six months when I was ten, has been a father to me in many ways.   9. YES... Tom is always interrupting me, which makes me mad.   10. NO   11. YES... To express the uselessness of worrying, Mark Twain once said, "I've had a lot of problems in my life, most of which never happened."

◇ **16 (p. 195):** 1. ... offers, **neither of which** I accepted.   2. ... three brothers, **two of whom** are professional athletes.   3. ... business ventures, **only one of which** is profitable.   4. ... fifty states, **the majority of which** are located....   5. The two women, **both of whom** are changing careers, have already dissolved....   6. ... success, **much of which** has been due to hard work, but **some of which** has been due to good luck.

◇ **17 (p. 195):** 1. Sally lost her job, which wasn't surprising.   2. She usually came to work late, which upset her boss.   3. So her boss fired her, which made her angry.   4. She hadn't saved any money, which was unfortunate.   5. So she had to borrow some money from me, which I didn't like.   6. She has found a new job, which is lucky.   7. So she has repaid the money she borrowed from me, which I appreciate.   8. She has promised herself to be on time for work every day, which is a good idea.

◇ **20 (p. 197):** 1. Only a few of the *movies* **shown at the Gray Theater** are suitable . . . .
2. *Jasmine*, **a viny plant with fragrant flowers,** grows only in warm places.
3. The *couple* **living in the house next door** are both college professors.
4. A throne is the *chair* **occupied by a queen, king, or other rulers.**
5. A knuckle is a *joint* **connecting a finger to the rest of the hand.**
6. We visited *Belgrade*, **the capital city of Yugoslavia.**
7. . . . by a huge *ice cap* **containing 70 percent of the earth's fresh water.**
8. *Astronomy*, **the study of planets and stars,** is one of the world's oldest sciences.
9. Only a small fraction of the *eggs* **laid by a fish** actually hatch and survive to adulthood.
10. Our solar system is in a *galaxy* **called the Milky Way.**
11. Two out of three *people* **struck by lightning** survive.
12. *Arizona*, **once thought to be a useless desert,** is today a rapidly growing . . . .
13. *Simon Bolivar*, **a great South American general,** led the fight for . . . .
14. . . . people enjoy *lemonade*, **a drink made of lemon juice, water, and sugar.**
15. . . . the sound of *laughter* **coming from the room next door to mine at the motel.**
16. Few tourists ever see a *jaguar*, **a spotted wild cat native to tropical America.**

◇ **21 (p. 198):** 1. . . . Martin Luther King, Jr., the leader of the . . . .   2. Neil Armstrong, the first person to set foot on the moon, reported . . . .   3. Susan B. Anthony, the first and only woman whose picture appears on U.S. money, worked tirelessly . . . .   4. (no commas)   5. . . . Abraham Lincoln, one of the truly great presidents of the United States, ran for public office 26 times and lost 23 of the elections. Walt Disney, the creator of Mickey Mouse and founder of his own movie production company, once got fired by a newspaper editor because he had no good ideas. Thomas Edison, the inventor of the light bulb and phonograph, was believed by his teachers to be too stupid to learn. Albert Einstein, one of the greatest scientists of all time, performed badly in almost all of his high school courses and failed his college entrance exam.

◇ **22 (p. 198):** 1. . . . Everest, the highest mountain in the world, is . . . .   2. . . . Baghdad, the capital of Iraq.   3. . . . seismographs, sensitive instruments that measure the shaking of the ground.   4. . . . Dead Sea, the lowest place on the earth's surface, is . . . . [NOTE: The shoreline of the Dead Sea is about 400 meters/1310 feet below sea level.]   5. . . . Buenos Aires, the capital of Argentina.   6. . . . lasers, devices that produce a powerful beam of light.   7. Mexico, the northernmost country in Latin America, lies . . . .   8. . . . Nigeria, the most populous country in Africa.   9. . . . Mexico City, the largest city in the Western Hemisphere, and New York City, the largest city in the United States, face . . . .   10. . . . mole, a small animal that spends its entire life underground, is almost blind. The aardvark, an African animal that eats ants and termites, also lives . . . .

◇ **26 (p. 201):** 1. . . . people **who(m)/that/Ø** I admire most is . . . .
2. . . . the only sport in which I am interested (*omit "in it"*). OR: . . . the only sport **which/that/Ø** I am interested in (*omit "it"*).
3. My favorite teacher, Mr. Peterson, (*omit "he"*) was always . . . .
4. . . . people in the government who **are** trying . . . .
5. . . . anyone who (*omit "he"*) wants to learn . . . . OR: . . . anyone **wanting** to learn . . . .
6. . . . Carver Hall, **which** is a large brick building . . . . OR: . . . Carver Hall, (*add comma, omit "that is"*) a large brick building . . . .
7. . . . a lot of people **waiting** in a long line . . . .
8. Students who **live** on campus . . . . OR: Students (*omit "who"*) **living** on campus . . . .
9. A myth is a story **which/that** expresses . . . . OR: A myth is a story **expressing** . . .

10. ...the librarian **who/that** sits at ... OR: the librarian **sitting** at ....

11. ... sister is Anna, **who** is 21 years old. OR: ... sister, Anna, is 21 years old.

12. ...in Sapporo, **which** is a city... OR: ...in Sapporo, (*omit "that is"*) a city....

13. Patrick, who is my oldest brother, is married and .... OR: Patrick, my oldest brother, is married and ....

14. The person **who sits/sitting** next to me is someone **who(m)/that/Ø** I've never met (*omit "him"*).

15. ... a small city (*omit "is"*) located .... OR: ... a small city **which/that** is located ....

◇ **PRACTICE TEST A (p. 202):** 1. D 2. A 3. B 4. D 5. B 6. A 7. C 8. D 9. C 10. A 11. C 12. B 13. C 14. D 15. D 16. B 17. D 18. B 19. A 20. C

Chapter 7: NOUN CLAUSES

◇ **1 (p. 206):** 1. Q(?) 2. N.Cl.(.) 3.Q(?) 4. N.Cl.(.) 5. Q(?) 6. N.Cl.(.) 7. N.Cl.(.) 8. Q(?) 9. Q(?) 10. N.Cl.(?) [NOTE: *"who she is" is a noun clause; the whole sentence is a question.*] 11. Q(?) 12. N.Cl.(.)

◇ **2 (p. 206):** 1. Where(?) 2. I don't know(.) 3. I don't know(.) 4. What(?) 5. How(?) 6. I don't know(.) 7. Where(?) 8. I don't know(.) 9. I don't know(.) 10. Why(?) 11. I don't know(.) 12. Who(?) 13. When (?) 14. I don't know(.) 15. Who(?) 16. I don't know(.)

◇ **3 (p. 207):** 1. When will Tom be here?... when Tom will be here. 2. Why is he coming?... why he is coming. 3. Which flight will he be on?... which flight he will be on. 4. Who is going to meet him at the airport?... who is going to meet him at the airport. 5. Who is Jim Hunter?... who Jim Hunter is. 6. What is Tom's address?... what Tom's address is. 7. Where does he live?... where he lives. 8. Where was he last week?... where he was last week. 9. How long has he been working for IBM?... how long he has been working for IBM? 10. What kind of computer does he have at home?... what kind of computer he has at home? 11. What does he need?... what he needs? 12. When did he call?... when he called. 13. What does he want to do after he gets here?... what he wants to do after he gets here? 14. Whose idea was it to have a party?... whose idea it was to have a party?

◇ **4 (p. 208):** 1. A: did Ruth go... B: Ruth went 2. A: He's looking for ... B: are you looking for 3. A: is my eraser ... B: it is 4. A: did he decide... B: he decided 5. A: is this ... B: it is 6. A: did he buy ... B: he bought 7. A: didn't Fred lock ... B: he didn't lock 8. A: have they been ... B: he and his family have lived ... 9. A: John's tutor is ... B: is John's tutor 10. A: you are taking ... B: are you taking 11. A: didn't you study ... B: I didn't study 12. A: are we supposed ... B: we're supposed

◇ **6 (p. 210):** 1. if/whether it will rain 2. when it will rain 3. if/whether Sam is 4. where Sam is 5. if/whether Jane called 6. what time Jane called 7. why the earth is called 8. how far it is 9. if/whether Susan has ever been 10. if/whether she speaks 11. who Ann played 12. who won 13. if/whether Ann won 14. if/whether all creatures, including fish and insects, feel 15. if/whether birds can communicate 16. how birds communicate 17. where the nearest post office is 18. if/whether there is a post office

◇ **7 (p. 212):** 1. Please tell me what **your name is.** 2. No one seems to know when **Maria will** arrive. 3. I wonder why **Bob was** late for class. 4. I don't know **what that word means.** 5. I wonder **if/whether the teacher knows** the answer. 6. What **they should** do about the hole in their roof is their most pressing problem. 7. I'll ask her **if/whether she would** like some coffee. 8. Be sure to tell the doctor where **it hurts**. 9. Why **I am** unhappy is

something I can't explain.   10. I wonder **if/whether** Tom knows about the meeting.
11. I need to know who **your teacher is**.   12. I don't understand why **the car is not** running
properly.

◇ **8 (p. 212):**   1. where to buy   2. whether to stay...go   3. how to fix   4. whether (or not) to look
5. where to get   6. whether (or not) to go   7. what time to pick   8. who to talk
9. whether to take...to do   10. how to solve   11. where to tell   12. how long to cook
13. what to wear   14. how much coffee to make   15. which essay to use   16. whether
to take...travel...(to) keep...save

◇ **10 (p. 214):**   1. *Regardless of the fact that I studied for three months for the examination,* I barely passed.
2. There's nothing we can do *about the fact that Jim lost our tickets to the concert.*   3. *The fact
that we are going to miss one of the best concerts of the year because of Jim's carelessness* makes me a
little angry.   4. *In view of the fact that we can't go to the concert,* let's plan to go to a movie.
5. *Except for the fact that I couldn't speak a word of Italian and understood very little,* I had a
wonderful time visiting my Italian cousins in Rome.   6. When I first visited Florida, I was
surprised *by the fact that many people living in Miami speak only Spanish.*   7. *The fact that Bobby
broke my grandmother's antique flower vase* isn't important.   8. *The fact that he lied about it* is
what bothers me.   9. At first, some of us objected *to the fact that Prof. Brown, who had almost
no teaching experience, was hired to teach the advanced physics courses,* but she has proven herself to
be one of the best.   10. I am impressed *by the fact that that automobile has the best safety record
of any car manufactured this year* and would definitely recommend that you buy that make.

◇ **11 (p. 214):**   1. The athlete said, **"W**here is my uniform?**"**
2. **"**Who won the game?**"** asked the spectator.
3. **"**Stop the clock,**"** shouted the referee. **"W**e have an injured player.**"**
4. **"**I can't remember,**"** Margaret said, **"**where I put my purse.**"**
5. Sandy asked her sister, **"H**ow can I help you get through this difficulty?**"**
6. **"**I'll answer your question later,**"** he whispered. **"I'**m trying to hear what the speaker is
saying.**"**
7. As the students entered the room, the teacher said, **"P**lease take your seats quickly.**"**
8. **"**Why did I ever take this job?**"** Barry wondered aloud.
9. After crashing into me and knocking all of my packages to the ground, the man stopped
abruptly, turned to me, and said softly, **"**Excuse me.**"**
10. **"**I'm going to rest for the next three hours,**"** she said. **"**I don't want to be disturbed.**"**
"That's fine,**"** I replied. **"Y**ou get some rest. I'll make sure no one disturbs you.**"**
11. **"**Do we want four more years of corruption and debt?**"** the candidate shouted into the
microphone.
"No!**"** the crowd screamed.
12.   The woman behind the fast-food restaurant counter shouted, **"W**ho's next?**"**
"I am,**"** three people replied all at the same time.
"Which one of you is really next?**"** she asked impatiently.
"I was here first,**"** said a young woman elbowing her way up to the counter. **"**I want a
hamburger.**"**
"You were not!**"** hollered an older man standing next to her. **"**I was here before you
were. **G**ive me a chicken sandwich and a cup of coffee.**"**
"Wait a minute! I was in line first,**"** said a young man. **"G**ive me a cheeseburger and a
chocolate shake.**"**
The woman behind the restaurant counter spotted a little boy politely waiting his turn.
She turned to him and said, **"H**i, Sonny. **W**hat can I get for you?**"**

◇ **12 (p. 216):**   1. was   2. needed   3. was having   4. had finished   5. had finished   6. would
arrive   7. was going to be/ would be   8. could solve   9. might come   10. might
come   11. had to leave   12. had to leave   13. should go   14. ought to go   15. to
stay   16. not to move   17. was   18. had arrived

◇ **13 (p. 216):** 1. if/whether she was planning   2. what time the movie begins   3. if/whether we could still get   4. how he can help   5. if/whether he could help   6. when the final decision would be made   7. where she had been   8. what Kim's native language is   9. what the problem was   10. if/whether I was doing   11. when this terrible drought is going   12. what time he had   13. who(m) she should give the message to   14. (that) we would be leaving   15. why we hadn't called

◇ **14 (p. 217):** 1. could still get . . . had already bought   2. had to clean up . . . empty . . . could leave . . . would   3. still smoked . . . had tried . . . didn't seem   4. was going . . . didn't know . . . worked   5. what the capital of Australia was/is . . . wasn't . . . thought it was   6. where the next chess match would take . . . hadn't been decided   7. would be . . . would . . . left   8. was . . . didn't think . . . would ever speak . . . was getting . . . would be speaking   9. . . . was pouring . . . had better take . . . would stop . . . didn't need   10. were . . . might be . . . could develop

◇ **18 (p. 221):**   1. What **the president is** going to say . . . .
   2. I asked Paul **to** help me . . . .
   3. My friend asked me, **"**What are you going to do Saturday?**"** I replied, **"**It depends on the weather.**"** OR: My friend asked me what **I was** going to do Saturday. I replied (that) it **depended** on the weather.
   4. What my friend and I did (*omit "it"*) was our secret. We . . . parents what **we did.**
   5. The doctor asked **if/whether** I felt okay. I told him that I **didn't** feel well.
   6. **It** is clear that the ability to use a computer (*omit "it"*) is an important skill . . . .
   7. They asked us **to be sure** (OR: **if we would** be sure) to turn out the lights when we leave/**left.**
   8. "Is **it** true you almost drowned?" my friend asked me.
      "Yes," I said. "I'm really glad to be alive. It was really frightening."
   9. **The** fact that I almost drowned makes . . . .

◇ **20 (p. 221):** 1. organize   2. be divided   3. call   4. be told   5. open   6. take   7. be   8. be mailed   9. obey   10. be given

◇ **21 (p. 222):** 1. whenever   2. wherever   3. whatever   4. whichever   5. whatever   6. who(m)ever   7. whichever   8. Whoever   9. whatever   10. wherever

◇ **PRACTICE TEST A (p. 223):** 1. B   2. C   3. B   4. D   5. A   6. A   7. D   8. D   9. A   10. B   11. B   12. A   13. D   14. D   15. D   16. B   17. C   18. C   19. A   20. B

Chapter 8: SHOWING RELATIONSHIPS BETWEEN IDEAS—PART I

◇ **1 (p. 226):** 1. fresh and sweet   2. apples and pears   3. washed and dried   4. am washing and drying   5. happily and quickly   6. biting and tasting   7. to bite and (to) taste   8. delicious but expensive   9. apples, pears, and bananas   10. red, ripe, and juicy

◇ **2 (p. 226):**   1. **I:** for his intelligence, cheerful disposition, and **honesty**
   2. **C:** was a lawyer and a politician
   3. **I:** she had to rent an apartment, make new friends, and **find** a job
   4. **C:** Barbara studies . . . and works
   5. **C:** is plentiful and relatively inexpensive
   6. **I:** enjoy visiting Disneyland and **touring** movie studios
   7. **C:** are usually interested in but a little frightened by
   8. **I:** Fainting can result from **either** a lack of oxygen or a loss of blood

9. **I**: how <u>to write</u> . . . , <u>organize</u> . . . , and **summarize**
10. **I**: <u>sailed</u> . . . <u>smoothly</u> and **quietly**
11. **C**: not <u>coffee</u> but <u>chocolate</u>
12. **I**: Not only <u>universities</u> **but also many government agencies** support medical . . . .
13. **C**: explains <u>why water freezes</u> and <u>how the sun produces heat</u>
14. **C**: need <u>light</u>, a <u>suitable climate</u>, and an ample <u>supply</u> ALSO: of <u>water</u> and <u>minerals</u>
15. **C**: With their keen <u>sight</u>, fine <u>hearing</u>, and refined <u>sense</u> of smell ALSO: hunt <u>day</u> or <u>night</u> ALSO: of <u>elk</u>, <u>deer</u>, <u>moose</u>, or <u>caribou</u>

◇ **3 (p. 227):** 1. knows 2. know 3. knows 4. know 5. know 6. wants 7. like 8. has 9. agrees 10. are 11. realizes 12. think

◇ **4 (p. 227):** 1. Many people drink **neither coffee nor alcohol**. 2. Barbara is fluent in **not only Chinese but also Japanese**. 3. I'm sorry to say that Paul has **neither patience nor sensitivity** to others. 4. She can **both sing and dance** 5. . . . you should talk to **either your teacher or your academic counselor**. OR: . . . talk **either to your teacher or to your academic counselor**. 6. Diana is **both intelligent and very creative**. 7. You may begin working **either tomorrow or next week**. 8. Michael told neither his **mother nor his father** . . . 9. . . . requires **not only balance and skill but also concentration and mental alertness**.

◇ **7 (p. 230):** 1. . . . cooking. **M**y wife . . . . 2. . . . cooking, [*optional comma*] but my wife . . . . 3. . . . that book. **I**t's very good. 4. . . . that book, but I didn't like it. 5. [*Add no punctuation.*] 6. . . . the door. **M**y sister answered . . . . 7. . . . the door, [*optional comma*] and my sister answered . . . . 8. . . . materials. **T**hey are found in rocks and soil. 9. . . . are minerals. **T**hey are found in rocks, soil, and water. 10. . . . by plane, [*optional comma*] or you can go . . . . 11. [*Add no punctuation.*] 12. . . . all night, so he declined . . . . 13. . . . invitation to dinner. **H**e needed to . . . . 14. . . . howling outside, yet it was warm and comfortable indoors. 15. . . . answer the phone, for I didn't want . . . . 16. . . . went camping. **I**t rained the entire time. 17. . . . under construction, so we had to take . . . . 18. . . . win the championship, yet our team won . . . . 19. . . . at the theatre late, but the play had not yet begun. **W**e were quite surprised. 20. . . . from one central place. **M**ost central heating systems service only one building, but some systems heat a group of buildings, such as those at a military base, a campus, or an apartment complex.

◇ **9 (p. 231):** 1. A hurricane's force begins to diminish <u>as soon as it strikes land</u>. 2. <u>When I reached my 21st birthday</u>, I didn't feel any older. 3. <u>Before I left for work</u>, I had a cup of tea. 4. I like to read the evening newspaper <u>after I get home from work</u>. 5. I have been late to work three times <u>since my watch broke</u>. 6. <u>Whenever it rains</u>, my cat hides under the house. 7. <u>Once I finish school</u>, I'm going to get a job. 8. I heard a gunshot <u>while I was waiting for my bus</u>. 9. <u>Until a new generator is installed</u>, the village will have no electric power. 10. I saw Mr. Wu <u>the last time I was in Taipei</u>. 11. I didn't have to stand in line at the airline counter <u>because I already had my boarding pass</u>. 12. <u>If the workplace is made pleasant</u>, productivity in a factory increases.

◇ **10 (p. 231):** 1. The lake was calm. Tom went fishing. 2. Because the lake was calm, Tom went fishing. 3. Tom went fishing because the lake was calm. **H**e caught two fish. 4. Tom went fishing because the lake was calm and caught two fish. 5. When Tom went fishing, the lake was calm. **H**e caught two fish. 6. The lake was calm, so Tom went fishing. **H**e caught two fish. 7. Because the lake was calm and quiet, Tom went fishing. 8. The lake was calm, quiet, and clear when Tom went fishing.

◇ **12 (p. 232):** 1. C 2. C 3. D 4. C 5. C 6. D 7. B 8. B 9. C 10. A 11. A 12. A 13. A 14. C 15. B

◇ **14 (p. 234):** 1. <u>As soon as the other passengers get on the bus,</u> we'll leave.   2. I turned off the lights <u>before I left the room.</u>   3. <u>Whenever Susan feels nervous,</u> she chews her nails.   4. <u>The first time I saw the great pyramids of Egypt in the moonlight,</u> I was speechless.   5. The frying pan caught on fire <u>while I was making dinner.</u>   6. <u>As soon as I finish working on the car,</u> we'll take a walk in the park.   7. <u>After Ceylon had been independent for 24 years,</u> its name was changed to Sri Lanka.   8. <u>By the time Shakespeare died in 1616,</u> he had written more than 37 plays.   9. <u>Since Douglas fell off his bicycle last week,</u> he has had to use crutches to walk.   10. Ms. Johnson will return your call <u>as soon as she has some free time.</u>   11. <u>Once John learns how to use a computer,</u> he'll be able to work more efficiently.   12. I won't return my book to the library <u>until I have finished my research project.</u>   13. Sue dropped a carton of eggs <u>as she was leaving the store.</u>   14. <u>The next time Sam goes to the movies,</u> he'll remember to take his glasses.   15. <u>When the flooding river raced down the valley,</u> it destroyed everything in its path.

◇ **16 (p. 235):** 1. A,B   2. B   3. A,D   4. B   5. C   6. A,B,C,D   7. B,C   8. C   9. A,D   10. B   11. D   12. A

◇ **17 (p. 236):** 1. We can go swimming every day *now that the weather is warm.*   2. *Since all of the students had done poorly on the test,* the teacher decided to give it again.   3. Cold air hovers near the earth *because it is heavier than hot air.*   4. *Because our TV set was broken,* we listened to the news on the radio.   5. *Now that Larry is finally caught up on his work,* he can start his vacation tomorrow.   6. *Inasmuch as you have paid for the theater tickets,* please let me pay for our dinner.   7. *Since 92,000 people already have reservations with Pan Am for a trip to the moon,* I doubt that I'll ever get the chance to go on one of the first tourist flights.   8. *As long as our flight is going to be delayed,* let's relax and enjoy a quiet dinner.   9. My registration is going to be canceled *because I haven't paid my fees.*   10. *Now that Erica has qualified for the Olympics in speedskating,* she must train even more vigorously.

◇ **18 (p. 237):** 1. because of   2. because   3. because   4. because of   5. Because of   6. Because   7. because   8. because of   9. because of   10. because   11. because   12. Because of

◇ **20 (p. 238):** 1. [*no changes*]   2. . . . wouldn't start. **Therefore,** he couldn't pick . . . .   3. . . . an inquisitive student, he was always . . . .   4 [*no changes*]   5. . . . our head. **Therefore,** it is important . . . .   6. . . . the eighth inning. **Therefore,** most of the audience . . . .   7. When I was in my teens and twenties, it was easy for me to get into an argument with my father because both of us . . . .   8. Robert did not pay close attention to what the travel agent said when he went to see her at her office last week. **Therefore,** he had to ask many of the same questions again the next time he talked to her.

◇ **21 (p. 238):** **Part I:** 1. Because   2. . . . rained. **Therefore,** we . . . .   3. because of   4. . . . town. **Therefore,** all . . . .   5. because of   6. Because the hurricane . . . town, all . . . .   7. because of   8. because   9. . . . courageous. Roman soldiers, **therefore,** ate . . . .
Part II: 1. Due to his poor eyesight, John . . . .   2. Since John has poor eyesight, he . . . .   3. . . . eyesight. Consequently, he . . . .   4. . . . heights. Consequently, she . . . .   5. due to   6. Since a camel . . . ten days, it is . . . .   7. . . . overweight. Consequently, his doctor . . . .   8. Since a diamond . . . hard, it can . . . .   9. Due to consumer demand for ivory, many . . . ruthlessly. Consequently, people who . . . .

◇ **22 (p. 239):** 1. so   2. such   3. so   4. so   5. such   6. such   7. so   8. so   9. so   10. such   11. so   12. so   13. So   14. so   15. such   16. so

◇ **24 (p. 241):** 1. (G) . . . I could listen to the news.   2. (I) . . . he can become a Canadian citizen.   3. (A) . . . she could read the fine print at the bottom of the contract.   4. (C) . . . she can fix her own car.   5. (H) . . . he will be considered for a promotion at this company.

6. (J)...she can graduate early.   7. (B)...he can travel in Europe.   8. (F)...it would not disturb her roommate.   9. (D)...she could see the dancers in the street.   10. (E) ...we can get expert advice on our itinerary.

◇ **27 (p. 243):** 1. Since opening....   2. ...before leaving the room.   3. While herding his goats....   4. Before marching into battle,....   5. After meeting/having met the movie star....   6. ...keys after searching through....   7. When first brought....   8. Since (being) imported into Australia many years ago, the rabbit....

◇ **28 (p. 244):** 1. [*no change*]   2. After stopping the fight, the police arrested two men and a woman.   3. Since opening his new business, Bob has been working 16 hours a day.   4. [*no change*]   5. While driving to work, Sam had a flat tire.   6. [*no change*]   7. [*no change*]   8. After working hard in the garden all afternoon, Tom took a shower and then went to the movies with his friends.   9. [*no change*]   10. [*no change*]   11. [*no change*]   12. Emily always straightens her desk before leaving the office at the end of the day.   13. [*no change*]

◇ **29 (p. 244):** 1. a. leaving . . . b. left   2. a. invented/had invented . . . b. inventing/having invented   3. a. working . . . b. was working   4. a. flies . . . b. flying   5. a. studied/had studied . . . b. studying/having studied   6. a. learning . . . b. learned   7. a. is taken . . . b. taken   8. a. taking . . . b. are taking   9. a. was driving . . . b. driving

◇ **30 (p. 245):** 1. **Keeping** one hand on the steering wheel, **Anna** opened a can of soda pop with her free hand.   2. [*no change*]   3. **Misunderstanding** the directions to the hotel, **I** arrived one hour late for the dinner party.   4. [*no change*]   5. **Misunderstanding** my directions to the hotel, **the taxi driver** took me to the wrong place.   6. **Living** a long distance from my work, **I** have to commute daily by train.   7. **Living** a long distance from her work, **Heidi** has to commute daily by train.   8. [*no change*]   9. **Picking** strawberries in the garden, **Martha** was stung by a bumblebee.   10. **Remembering** that she hadn't turned off the oven, **Ann** went directly home.   11. **Tripping** on the carpet, **Jim** spilt his coffee.   12. **Having recognized** his face but having forgotten his name, **I** just smiled and said, "Hi."   13. [*no change*]   14. **Lying** by the swimming pool, **I** realized I was getting sunburned.   15. [*no change*]   16. **Living** in the Pacific Northwest, where it rains a great deal, **my family and I** are accustomed to cool, damp weather.

◇ **31 (p. 246):** 1. E   2. J   3. A   4. G   5. B   6. L   7. I   8. H   9. C   10. K   11. F   12. D

◇ **33 (p. 247):** 1. Upon arriving at the airport ....   2. Upon reaching the other side of the lake ....   3. Upon discovering it was hot ....   4. Upon hearing my name called ....   5. Upon hearing those words ....   6. upon investigating the cause ....   7. Upon learning the problem was not at all serious ....   8. Upon being told that she had gotten (had got) it ....

◇ **34 (p. 248):** 1. After spending some time in a cocoon, a caterpillar ....   2. [*no change*]   3. Upon entering the theater, we handed....   4. Being unprepared/Unprepared for the test, I didn't do well.   5. Before leaving on my trip, I checked....   6. [*no change*]   7. Not having understood/Not understanding the directions, I got lost.   8. My father reluctantly agreed to let me attend the game after having talked/after talking it over with my mother.   9. Upon discovering I had lost my key to the apartment, I called....   10. [*no change*]   11. Garcia Lopez de Cardenas accidentally discovered the Grand Canyon while looking for....   12. [*no change*]   13. After having waited/After waiting for over a half an hour, we were finally....   14. Before getting accepted on her country's Olympic running team, Maria had spent....   15. Not paying attention to his driving, George didn't see ....

◇ **36 (p. 250):** 1. **I**   2. **C**   3. **I**   4. **C**   5. **I**   6. **I**   7. **I**   8. **C**   9. **I**   10. **C**   11. **I**   12. **I**   13. **I**   14. **I**   15. **C**

◇ **37 (p. 251):**   1. I was very tired, **so I went** to bed.
2. Because our leader could not attend the meeting, (*omit "so"*) it was canceled. OR: (*omit "Because"*) Our leader could not attend the meeting, so it was canceled.
3. **My wife and I like** to travel.
4. I always fasten my seatbelt before **starting/I start** the engine.
5. I don't like our classroom **b**ecause it is hot and crowded. I hope we can change . . . .
6. The day was very warm and humid, **so** I turned on the air conditioner.
7. Upon **learning** that my car couldn't be repaired for three days, I **was** very distressed.
8. **Because I (had)** missed the final examination, the teacher gave me a failing grade.
9. Both my sister and my brother **are** going to be at the family reunion.
10. I hope my son will remain in school until he **finishes** his degree.
11. My brother has succeeded in business because (*omit "of"*) he works hard.
12. Luis stood up, turned toward me, and **spoke** so softly that I couldn't hear what he said.
13. I was lost. I could find **neither** my parents **nor** my brother.
14. When I traveled through Europe**,** I visited England, France, Italy, Germany, and **Switzerland.**

◇ **PRACTICE TEST A (p. 252):**   1. B   2. A   3. B   4. D   5. C   6. D   7. A   8. C   9. B
10. A   11. B   12. C   13. A   14. A   15. B   16. D   17. A   18. C
19. C   20. C

Chapter 9: SHOWING RELATIONSHIPS BETWEEN IDEAS—PART II

◇ **1 (p. 255):**   1. even though   2. because   3. Even though   4. Because   5. even though
6. because   7. Even though   8. because   9. even though   10. Even though . . .
because   11. even though   12. even though . . . because   13. Even though . . . because

◇ **3 (p. 256):**   **Part I**: 1. Nevertheless   2. but   3. even though   4. but   5. Nevertheless   6. Even
though   7. even though   8. but   9. nevertheless   10. Nevertheless
Part II: 11. However   12. yet   13. Although   14. yet   15. Although
16. However   17. although   18. yet   19. However   20. However

◇ **4 (p. 257):**   1. . . . good advice. **N**evertheless, she . . . .   2. . . . good advice**,** but she . . . .   3. Even
though . . . good advice**,** she . . . .   4. . . . good advice. **S**he did not follow it, however.
5. Thomas was thirsty. **I** offered him some water. **H**e refused it.   6. [*no change*]
7. Thomas was thirsty. **H**e, nevertheless, refused the glass of water I brought him.
8. Thomas was thirsty**,** yet he refused to drink the water that I offered him.

◇ **5 (p. 258):**
1.	a. Even though	2.	a. In spite of	3.	a. Despite	4.	a. In spite of
	b. Despite		b. Although		b. Although		b. Even though
	c. Despite		c. Although		c. Despite		c. In spite of
	d. Despite		d. In spite of		d. Although		d. even though
	e. Even though		e. In spite of		e. Despite		e. in spite of
							f. even though
							g. even though
							h. in spite of

◇ **6 (p. 259):**   1. B   2. E   3. J   4. F   5. C   6. H   7. A   8. G   9. I   10. D

◇ **7 (p. 260):**   1. C   2. D   3. C   4. C   5. B   6. B

◇ **9 (p. 260):**   1. B   2. A   3. B   4. B   5. D   6. C   7. B   8. B   9. A   10. C

◇ **13 (p. 264):** 1. In case you need...with me, I'll....   2. We'll...in case you need to call us.
3. You'd better...with you in case the weather changes.   4. ...design project. In case you find that you need help with it, she'll be....   5. My boss...in case the company ....
6. In case I'm not back to make dinner, I put the ....   7. In the event that Janet... tomorrow, she will....   8. You'd better...in the event that you run out....   9. My family...the country in the event that there is a civil war.   10. ...safe side, I always... carry-on bag in the event that the airline loses....   11. In the event that there is no airport bus, you can always....   12. ...evening. She has already...speech in the event that she wins it tonight.

◇ **14 (p. 264):** 1. B   2. A   3. A   4. B   5. B   6. A   7. A   8. B   9. B   10. A   11. A
12. B

◇ **15 (p. 265):** 1. not going to go   2. rains   3. pass   4. only if   5. always eat   6. even if
7. gets   8. won't   9. don't wake   10. if   11. Don't borrow   12. are still some

◇ **16 (p. 266):** 1. Only if you help me can I finish this work on time.   2. If you help me, I can finish this work on time.   3. Only if I am invited will I go.   4. If I am invited, I will go.   5. Only if I am hungry do I eat.   6. If I am hungry during the morning, I usually eat some fruit.
7. Only if you know both Arabic and Spanish will you be considered for that job.   8. Only if the refrigerator is empty will John go to the market.   9. Only if you promise not to get angry will I tell you the truth about what happened.   10. If you get angry, I won't discuss it any further.

◇ **18 (p. 267):** 1. You should (had better/have to/must) eat less and get more exercise. Otherwise, you won't lose weight.   2. The children have to (had better/should/must) finish all of their chores. Otherwise, they cannot watch....   3. You have to (must/should/had better) speak up now. Otherwise, the boss will go ahead....   4. You must (had better/should/have to) stop at the store on your way home from work. Otherwise, we won't have anything....   5. You had better (have to/should/must) think it through very carefully. Otherwise, you won't come up with....   6. We have to (had better/should/must) catch fish this morning. Otherwise, we're going to have beans....   7. You should (had better/have to/must) get someone to help you. Otherwise, it's going to be very....   8. Maria had better (should/has to/must) find a way to convince the boss that the error was unavoidable. Otherwise, she'll probably lose her job.

◇ **19 (p. 267):** 1. passes   2. doesn't pass   3. passes   4. passes   5. doesn't pass   6. passes
7. passes   8. doesn't pass   9. must/has to pass   10. had better (must/has to) pass

◇ **21 (p. 268):** 1. B   2. D   3. D   4. A   5. C   6. B   7. B   8. C   9. B   10. A   11. C
12. D   13. A   14. D   15. B   16. C   17. D   18. A   19. D   20. B
21. D   22. A

◇ **28 (p. 275):** 1. Government money is essential to successful research at our university. For example, much of the research in the medical school is funded by government grants. **Moreover/In addition / Furthermore,** such departments as physics, chemistry, computer science, and engineering now rely increasingly on govenment funding.
2. Applicants for the position must fulfill certain requirements. They need a college degree and two years' experience in the field. **In addition (Furthermore/Moreover),** they must have computer skills. **Furthermore (Moreover/In addition),** two letters of recommendation should be submitted along with the application.
3. There are several reasons why I write in my diary every day. Writing in a diary allows me to reflect on a day's events and their meanings. As the Greek philosopher Plato said, ''A life that is unexamined is not worth living.'' **In addition (Furthermore/Moreover)** I like the idea of keeping a record of my life to share with my children at a later date. **Furthermore (In addition/Moreover),** writing in a diary is calming. It forces me to take time out of my busy day to rest and think quiet thoughts.

4. If you are interested in the arts, you should come to visit my city, Montreal. Montreal is a leading cultural center in North America. You can go to the Museum of Fine Arts to see displays of works by Canadian artists, past and present. **Moreover (In addition/Furthermore),** Montreal has a world famous symphony orchestra and numerous theaters. One of them, the International Theater, performs plays in several languages.

◇ PRACTICE TEST A (p. 277): 1. C   2. D   3. D   4. B   5. A   6. D   7. B   8. C   9. D
10. C   11. C   12. A   13. B   14. A   15. C   16. D   17. B   18. B
19. A   20. B

Chapter 10: CONDITIONAL SENTENCES

◇ **1 (p. 280):**
1. a. yes
   b. no
2. a. no
   b. yes
   c. no
3. a. yes
   b. no
   c. yes
4. a. yes
   b. no
   c. no
5. a. no
   b. yes
6. a. no
   b. yes
7. a. yes
   b. no
8. a. yes
   b. no
9. a. no
   b. no
   c. yes

◇ **2 (p. 281):** 1. were...would take   2. floats/will float   3. were...would not exist   4. doesn't arrive   5. were...wouldn't want   6. consisted...would be   7. were...would call...(would) talk   8. travels...always spends   9. would human beings live... were   10. disappears/will disappear   11. had...would have to...would not be

◇ **3 (p. 282):** 1. had told...would have given   2. had used...would have received   3. had realized...wouldn't have made   4. had known...wouldn't have voted   5. had read...wouldn't have washed   6. B: would have come...(would have) washed... had asked...   A: would have come...had called   7. had written...wouldn't have lost   8. would you have taken...had known

◇ **4 (p. 283):** 1. had...wouldn't have to   2. send   3. would have suffered   4. Would people be...had   5. would we use...didn't have (possible: hadn't)   6. felt...would drop   7. doesn't rain...will die...die...will go   8. had brought...would not have had   9. had been invented...would have been interviewed   10. discover...will call   11. had known...would have stayed up...(would have) finished   12. had not collided...would not have become...would be...still existed...would be

◇ **5 (p. 284):** 1. If I hadn't been sick yesterday, I would have gone to class.   2. If Alan ate breakfast, he wouldn't overeat at lunch.   3. Peter would have finished unloading the truck if John had helped him.   4. Jack wouldn't have been late to his own wedding if his watch hadn't been ten minutes slow.   5. I would ride the bus to work every morning if it weren't always so crowded.   6. I would have brought extra money with me if you had told me we were going to dinner after the movie.   7. If Sam had known that highway 57 was closed, he would have taken an alternative route.   8. If I hadn't lost my key, I wouldn't have had to pound on the door to wake my roommate when I got home last night.

◇ **8 (p. 285):** 1. weren't raining...would finish   2. had eaten...wouldn't be   3. hadn't left...would have   4. would have answered...hadn't been studying   5. hadn't been shining... wouldn't have gone   6. wouldn't ache...hadn't played   7. wouldn't stop... weren't running   8. had eaten...wouldn't have to have   9. hadn't been playing... would have heard   10. weren't closing...wouldn't have to leave

◇ **9 (p. 286):** 1. If the wind **weren't blowing** hard, I **would take** the boat out for a ride.   2. I **wouldn't feel** better now if you **hadn't talked** to me about my problems last night.   3. If Gary **hadn't carried** heavy furniture when he helped Ann move, his back **wouldn't hurt** now.   4. If Paul **weren't working** on two jobs right now, he **would have time** to help you with your remodeling. 5. If I **had been working** at the restaurant last night, I **would have waited** on your table. 6. If Diane **hadn't asked questions** every time she didn't understand a problem, she **wouldn't have** a good understanding of geometry now.   7. If a bulldozer **hadn't been blocking** the road, we **would have arrived** on time.   8. She **wouldn't be** exhausted today if she **had gotten** some sleep last night.   9. If they **had been paying** attention, they **would have seen** the sign marking their exit from the highway.   10. If the doctor really **cared** about his patients, he **would have explained** the medical procedure to me before surgery.

◇ **11 (p. 287):** 1. Should you need   2. Were I you   3. Had they realized   4. Had Alan tried 5. Should anyone call   6. Were I   7. Had everyone arrived   8. Should the post office close   9. Had I not opened   10. Were she   11. Should you change   12. had she been

◇ **13 (p. 288):** 1. I hadn't twisted my ankle   2. I had not forgotten to tell him that she needed a ride 3. you hadn't helped me   4. he had told his boss about the problem   5. I hadn't opened the door slowly   6. the woman behind me hadn't started yelling impatiently at him to check her out   7. I hadn't wanted everyone to know about it   8. his boss had given him the time off   9. the building weren't locked   10. Marge hadn't given us the benefit of her expertise   11. she hadn't driven straight to the garage when the engine started making loud noises   12. hadn't made the cast stay to rehearse some troublesome parts of the play

◇ **14 (p. 289):** 1. A   2. A   3. D   4. D   5. C   6. A   7. C   8. A   9. C   10. A 11. C   12. A   13. B   14. A   15. A   16. A   17. B   18. B   19. A   20. C

◇ **18 (p. 293):** 1. were shining   2. had gone   3. had driven   4. could swim   5. would stop 6. had won   7. had gotten   8. hadn't quit   9. were   10. would sing   11. could bring   12. had offered

◇ **19 (p. 293):** 1. hadn't missed   2. would stop . . . were shining   3. hadn't gone . . . had studied 4. hadn't moved . . . had taken   5. would stop   6. hadn't paid   7. would hurry . . . would relax   8. hadn't invited   9. would tell   10. had worn (*also possible:* were wearing) . . . had realized   11. hadn't been elected . . . hadn't voted   12. could buy . . . grew 13. weren't . . . were . . . were . . . were   14. would meet . . . disagreed . . . could prove

◇ **21 (p. 295):** 1. were   2. had been made   3. had (never) met   4. were   5. hadn't heard 6. didn't have (OR: hadn't)   7. didn't exist   8. had happened   9. were 10. were   11. had stopped   12. had appeared

◇ **PRACTICE TEST A (p. 297):** 1. B   2. C   3. C   4. A   5. C   6. B   7. D   8. B   9. D 10. A   11. C   12. B   13. B   14. B   15. D   16. C   17. D   18. D 19. D   20. A